FAREWELL,
Town of Streetsville

The Year Before Amalgamation

Tom Urbaniak

FAREWELL,
TOWN OF STREETSVILLE
The Year Before Amalgamation

Tom Urbaniak

Epic Press

Belleville, Ontario, Canada

FAREWELL, TOWN OF STREETSVILLE
THE YEAR BEFORE AMALGAMATION

Canadian Cataloguing in Publication Data

Urbaniak, Tom, 1976–
      Farewell, Town of Streetsville: the year before amalgamation

Includes bibliographical references and index.
ISBN 1-55306-353-8

    1. Streetsville (Mississauga, Ont.)—History. 2. Streetsville (Mississauga, Ont.)—Politics and government. 3. McCallion, Hazel, 1921–
I. Title.

FC3099.S78U73 2002	971.3'535	C2002-900280-X
F1059.5.S79U73 2002		

The author can be contacted at urbaniak@sympatico.ca

Cover painting by Marilyn Kutsukake
Back cover photograph by Stephen Uhraney

Epic Press is an imprint of *Essence Publishing*,
44 Moira Street West, Belleville, Ontario, Canada K8P 1S3.
Phone: 1-800-238-6376. Fax: (613) 962-3055.
E-mail: info@essencegroup.com
Internet: www.essencegroup.com

Printed in Canada
by

E**p**ic
Press

DEDICATED TO
THOSE WHO SEE COMMUNITIES
AS MORE THAN BUILDINGS,
PUT PEOPLE BEFORE PROFITS,
AND REGARD CIVIC AFFAIRS
AS A WAY TO GIVE SOMETHING BACK.

Table
of Contents

Preface

This is the story of a community with a heart, a municipality that valued its civic spirit, a town where people were citizens and not simply consumers.

This book examines Streetsville in 1973, the year before it was amalgamated with the towns of Mississauga and Port Credit to form the City of Mississauga. Earlier events, including the perennial discussions on local government restructuring, are highlighted to adequately present the context for what transpired in 1973. Here we also meet Hazel McCallion, one of Canada's best-known and longest-serving municipal leaders, in an early phase of her political career.

The reader is left to reflect on several issues, including the impact of grassroots civic participation; the calibre of the town's governance and management (and the changes thereto during the 1960s and early 1970s); the extent of the connection between municipal status and community identity; as well as the manner in which a regional government was constituted for Peel.

The year before amalgamation was important for reasons not directly related to the resistance to the merger plans. The first Streetsville Bread and Honey Festival was held that year. There were significant, proactive downtown regeneration efforts. The election campaign for the first Mississauga city council, with Streetsville as Ward 9, was a watershed event with a dramatic outcome. Moreover, after the town's fate was sealed, its elected officials, administrators, and citizen volunteers faced the important task of effecting a smooth and fair transition, punctuated by activities to officially bid farewell to Streetsville as a municipal entity. This book also looks at these aspects of what was probably the busiest year in the town's history.

The "reform" or "neighbourhood" ethos, which rose to prominence in some Canadian communities (mostly cities) in the late 1960s and early 1970s, played a crucial role in Streetsville. It embraced most segments of the community, although many middle-class professionals and some small-businesspeople appear to have been especially active. This reform phenomenon—not reactionary parochialism—appears to have been closely associated with the opposition to amalgamation. Public support for (or acquiescence in the face of) relentless development had given way to a "planning for people" orientation, with a greater emphasis on collective well-being, including conservation of green space, public input/participation in development planning, preservation or rejuvenation of historically and architecturally significant sites, as well as improved community amenities.

The reform ethos represented, in many respects, a marriage of toryism (the *philosophy*, not to be confused with the political party or with neo-conservatism) and progressive activism. There was a determination to preserve a sense of community, as well as to bring changes to a policy process that many regarded as dominated by insensitive, large, private interests. Streetsville's council and administration, in contrast with their counterparts in the much-larger neighbouring municipality (the Town of Mississauga), were perceived as being very much in tune with this new political climate.

Indeed, it can be argued that, during its last several years as a municipality, Streetsville was home to what respected American urban political scientist Clarence Stone labels a "middle class progressive regime." Such a regime is not the norm. More common are "development regimes," where members of the corporate elite are key players in the informal local "governing coalition." Progressive regimes, argues Stone, require an attentive and civically active citizenry, not to mention a broad consensus about the paramountcy of quality-of-life (as opposed to purely economic) issues.[1]

*   *   *

I do not live in Streetsville, and I was born after 1973. As a Mississauga resident, I do, however, have a longstanding respect and appreciation for Streetsville. In 1997, I became especially interested in the community's battle to retain its municipal status when I prepared an article entitled "The Year the People Lost Their Town"[2] for the *Mississauga Booster* (now the *Streetsville/Meadowvale Booster*), where I have worked part-time since 1996 while attending university. By the summer of 1998, I had decided to further pursue this research on my own time.

Many people assisted along the way. I am grateful to them, while accepting full responsibility for any errors or shortcomings. I tip my hat to the staff of the Ontario Archives, especially Wayne Crockett and Mark Epp; to the Region of Peel Archives, especially Diane Kuster and Rowena Cooper; to the staff at the Ruth Konrad Collection of Canadiana at the Mississauga Central Library, particularly Dorothy Kew; to Norm Potts, president of the Streetsville Historical Society, for allowing me access to the society's archives and records, housed in Streetsville's former jail; to Bob Keeping, for

providing me with various valuable sound recordings; and to Doug
Flowers, Jim Graham, Emmaleen Sabourin, and Don Fletcher for
lending me various documents from the early 1970s.

I am deeply indebted to Marilyn Kutsukake for her painting,
prepared especially for this book's cover, of Streetsville's town hall
as it looked in 1973.

The 46 individuals who were interviewed were all forthcoming and very helpful.[3] I enjoyed immensely my often-lengthy discussions with them. Most of their names appear in the endnotes
and/or the main text.

A big expression of thanks is extended to Jean Watt, retired editor of the *Booster* and a lifelong Streetsville resident, for her advice
and for her comments on drafts of this book. Jean has been perhaps
my most enthusiastic supporter throughout this process. She seems
to know almost every current and former resident of Streetsville. On
countless occasions, she has been able to tell me where I can reach
particular individuals.

Last, but certainly not least, I sincerely acknowledge the
members of my family for their ongoing interest, support, and
encouragement.

—Tom Urbaniak
Mississauga, Ontario
December 2001

PART I

Streetsville and Its Struggle

1 | Streetsville, 1973

"I don't know whether you know Mariposa," wrote Stephen Leacock in *Sunshine Sketches of a Little Town*. "If not, it is of no consequence, for if you know Canada at all, you are probably acquainted with a dozen towns just like it."[1]

Streetsville, like fictional Mariposa,* was in many ways a typical Ontario town. But just as no two human beings are completely alike, each community has an identity, strengths and weaknesses, and reasons to be proud or ashamed. Its character is influenced by its past, its triumphs and adversities, its wealth or poverty, its friends and detractors, its goals and aspirations, and by the little corner of the world in which it happens to be situated.

The Town of Streetsville—about 7,200 persons strong in 1973[2]—was a geographically compact community, covering a small portion (1,089 acres) of the Credit River Valley. It had witnessed numerous changes during the preceding 50 years. The post-World

---

* Many of Leacock's contemporaries in Orillia, Ontario, were convinced, however, that they were the ones being portrayed (and often not in a flattering manner).

War II period had been a time of significant growth, during which Streetsville's population increased ten-fold. New subdivisions outnumbered the gracious old homes. Although the rate of growth decreased during the early 1960s, this was only temporary. In the early 1970s, Markborough Properties commenced development of the Meadowvale community, part of which was situated in Streetsville,* and major plans were afoot for the Erin Mills community, which was to graze the southern and western parts of the town. In 1968, when the municipality commissioned an important study of its boundaries, almost all the land surrounding the community was owned by large developers. Markborough was controlled by various financial interests, and the Erin Mills project was being spearheaded by Canadian Equity and Development, which was started in 1953 by E.P. Taylor to develop the suburban Don Mills community. When the company went public in 1968, Cadillac and Fairview corporations (which merged in 1974) bought most of the shares.[3]

---

* Described as "A New Town in the Country," Meadowvale was slated to occupy 3,000 acres. A $250,000 information pavilion greeted drivers exiting Highway 401 to Mississauga Road. Nearby Erin Mills was also assessed very favourably by the Mississauga press. Although some urban analysts were already critical of the suburban "new towns" for creating cold, impersonal neighbourhoods which were not often amenable to pedestrians and transit users, this thinking had not permeated conventional planning practices. Also noteworthy are the "restrictive covenants" which Markborough required home buyers to follow. These very strict, company-imposed 40-year rules "legislated out" certain property uses (like running a home-based business, unless you were a doctor or dentist) and stipulated that, "Before any buildings, fences, or hedges of any kind can be erected the plans, dimensions, elevation, specification, colours and materials must first be approved by our Markborough project staff to ensure compliance with the overall objectives of the community environment." See "Meadowvale: A New Town in the Country" (Markborough brochure, c. 1970, Toronto Urban Affairs Library) and "Protective Covenants" (April 1975, Toronto Urban Affairs Library).

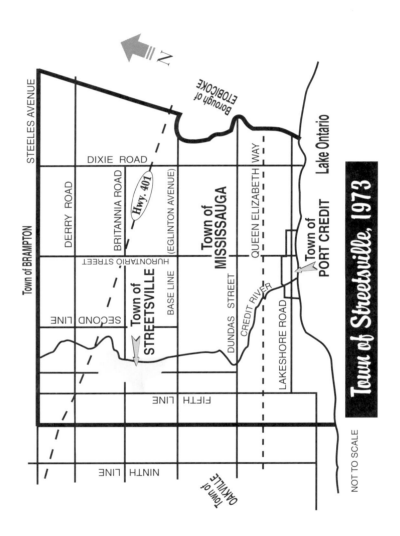

Some things had still not changed, however. Elizabeth Colley, Streetsville's librarian in 1973, recalls "a lovely community surrounded by cattle farms."[4] This is consistent with Millie Lundy's 1957 reflections: "Is it any wonder that I love Streetsville and that when I look around and see the beauty of hills and valleys, river and creek and trees and sky I know it is the finest spot in the world to live[?]"[5]

Many people who settled in Streetsville in the 1950s and 1960s quickly developed an affinity for its engaging, friendly atmosphere. Some of these families had once lived in Toronto. Commuting to the city was not uncommon, and traffic jams were less frequent in 1973 than today; much of the drive was through still-sparse countryside. The distance to downtown Toronto was about 30 kilometres, and the town was situated just south of the Macdonald-Cartier Freeway (Highway 401). The international airport was 10 kilometres away. During the 1950s, many Streetsville residents worked at A.V. Roe or Orenda Corporations near the airport in Malton. Some of the neighbourhoods which were built in Streetsville during that era were commonly referred to as "Avro subdivisions."

The welcome received by new residents was usually warm and genuine. Neighbours would often go out of their way to greet the newcomers. Municipal officials would strike up conversations. Parishioners from the applicable denomination would call.

Al Betts, president of the Streetsville and District Chamber of Commerce in 1973, moved to Streetsville in the mid-1950s. He remembers his first visit to a local hardware store: "'You're new in town, aren't you?' the merchant enquired. We started talking. When I came out of that store, I could care less about whether I got home [quickly] or not. I was so laid back, and I knew then that this was the place in which I wanted to live. All that hustle and bustle had just been taken away from me."[6]

In a 1972 letter to Premier Bill Davis, Streetsville resident Billie Field succinctly summarized the oft-expressed sentiments of those who had moved to the community:

> Having lived in large cities most of our lives, we are well aware of the impersonal attitudes that exist between the various civic services and the recipients, however, upon arrival in Streetsville, the attitude of a small town was highly apparent—the feeling of informality, the realization that the police force is truly there to serve young and old, rich and poor ... that the civic services were fulfilled quickly without consideration to a person's social position, that the people themselves go out of their way to ensure that you quickly become a responsible addition to their town.[7]

A LOOK BACK

The area had a rich history. By the early 1700s, the Credit Valley was the territory of the Ojibwa people, who had taken it over from the Iroquois. Contact between the Ojibwa and Europeans became more frequent after the British victory in the North American theatre of the Seven Years' War, and especially after the arrival of Loyalists during and after the American Revolution. In an 1805 treaty, the Mississaugas (as the Ojibwa of the region had come to be called by the Europeans) ceded much of their southern Credit Valley territory. The northern tracts, including what is now Streetsville, were included in an 1818 document.

With the land open to European settlement, Timothy Street, after whom the community is named, began surveying the area, and a few entrepreneurs quickly sensed opportunities. By the mid-1820s, Street himself had brought his family from St. David's (on the Niagara peninsula) to settle near the Credit River. His permanent home, constructed in 1825, still stands on Mill Street. It is the oldest brick edifice in Peel.

Streetsville had its own post office by 1828, and after a few more years it was a thriving local centre of industry, largely because of its mills. The weekly newspaper, the *Streetsville Review*, was founded in 1846. It was one of the first regular publications between Toronto and Windsor, and it was still around in the 1970s to witness the amalgamation.

In 1857, Streetsville withdrew from the Township of Toronto, and was formally incorporated in 1858. Its population at the time was perhaps 1,500, but within 20 years it fell to about 700. The railway had initially bypassed Streetsville, and when the Credit Valley Railway was finally completed through the village in 1879, it was too late; the community's population remained stagnant for another seven decades.

The post-World War II years saw rapid economic growth, including a baby boom, an expanding middle class, and a major increase in the number of private automobiles. These factors, combined with Streetsville's proximity to Toronto, stimulated an increase in population and commercial activity. The official program for Streetsville's 1953 Coronation Day festivities acknowledged that things would never be the same:

> Since early in this century, Streetsville has moved forward slowly, with changes coming almost imperceptibly. It has not been swept into industrialization. However, the changing patterns of living are having their effect upon the village—industries are coming in and several housing developments are underway. It is evident that Streetsville is 'on the march' to greater things and that a brighter future lies ahead for this pioneer settlement that is ... so well located.[8]

The 1941 annual report of the Streetsville Public Library showed a local population of 700. Less than two decades later, in 1959, when Streetsville celebrated its centennial (one year late) as an incorporated community, its residents numbered 4,124.[9]

Three years after that, its population having surpassed 5,000, the Village of Streetsville became the Town of Streetsville.

A VIBRANT CIVIC LIFE

In her *History of Streetsville*, a short book published for the first Bread and Honey Festival in 1973, Mary Manning praised the "levelheadedness" of the civic leaders for maintaining a stable, pleasant community despite the growth.[10] Whether or not the leaders deserve the credit, Streetsville was a very vibrant place in 1973. It had clubs and associations of every description—a Rotary Club and Rotaryanns, Kinsmen and Kinettes, Lions and Lionesses, an active Senior Citizens' Club, Catholic Women's League, Independent Order of Odd Fellows (who celebrated their 100th anniversary in Streetsville in 1973), Masons, Order of the Eastern Star, and a Women's Institute. The Royal Canadian Legion, Branch 139, had a large and dedicated membership. These organizations were complemented by more-recently established neighbourhood and residents' associations. The Streetsville Neighbours' Assistance Program (SNAP) was a group of volunteers who assisted ill, elderly, and shut-in residents, as well as those experiencing bereavement or other family crises. There was even an environmental club, known as SAVE (Streetsville Against a Vanishing Environment), which organized local projects like recycling drives and called on people to alter their lifestyles by, among other things, carpooling and reducing waste.[11]

Streetsville had a popular horticultural society. A club for gardening enthusiasts was formed in 1914, but became inactive in 1954. It was revived in 1972, thanks primarily to the efforts of librarian Elizabeth Colley. It quickly generated the interest of at least a few dozen enthusiastic gardeners.[12]

The Streetsville Historical Society was formed in 1970, at the insistence of town council, to "preserve, collect and make available for research items reflecting various aspects of the community's history...."[13]

For young people, there were Brownies and Girl Guides, or Cubs, Scouts, Venturers, and Rovers. The cadet groups included the Army Cadets, the Navy League, and the Royal Canadian Sea Cadets. For youths who were of a more musical persuasion, there was the popular Streetsville Chorus under the direction of Gary Clipperton.

Streetsville boasted a wide-ranging sports scene. Hockey was enormously popular, as it was in many Canadian small towns. The Streetsville Derbys, an Ontario Junior A Hockey Association club, enjoyed a very loyal following. The Streetsville Minor Hockey Association had teams for males and females. There was also minor soccer, softball, a bowling league, baseball and t-ball, a judo club, lacrosse, a figure skating club, and more. The Streetsville Lawn Bowling Club (founded in 1890) and the square-dancing club drew somewhat older participants. Courses were available locally in everything from tennis to horseback riding.[14]

The Streetsville and District Chamber of Commerce was a recognized and respected entity, consisting mostly of small-business owners, including downtown retailers and professionals who had their practices in town. Many members of the chamber were also active on service clubs or associated with other local volunteer endeavours. Although some residents have skeptically commented that the chamber was most visible at election time, because it was known to occasionally set up committees to ensure that there would not be acclamations,[15] the organization did organize several ongoing community initiatives, such as the trade fairs and the annual Miss Streetsville pageant. In the spring of 1973, it would be called upon to assume an active role in co-ordinating the Streetsville Bread and Honey Festival.

Streetsville had a large Portuguese population in 1973—

between 600 and 800 people.* Most of the Portuguese-speaking residents were from the Azores Islands, especially Sao Miguel. They had moved to the area after 1955, when Joe Mota led the way to Streetsville,[16] and many worked in local industries. In 1971, several members of the Portuguese community, in co-operation with Father Henry Kea ("Padre Eurico") of St. Joseph's Parish (who, although of Dutch descent, was able to speak Portuguese because of his previous missionary work in Brazil), formed the Portuguese Canadian Integration Movement. It quickly became a prominent, multi-faceted organization under the energetic leadership of Jose (Joe) Simoes. The organization's executive actively opposed amalgamation. In one of his letters to Premier Bill Davis, Simoes insisted that, "The Town of Streetsville has provided a good home for our people. Our Council has been good to us in our efforts."[17] He repeated these opinions when interviewed for this book.

The municipality helped to organize English classes. There was a modest Portuguese-language collection at the Streetsville Library, and local recreation officials were reviewing how services could be more readily accessed by the Portuguese-speaking residents of Streetsville.[18] A major three-day festival, started by Portuguese res-

---

* Statistics Canada's 1971 data for census tracts in the Toronto area contains 11 headings for ethnic groups. "Portuguese" is not among them. However, for the Streetsville census tract, the total number of residents classified under the 11 headings is 6,195, out of a Streetsville population of 6,840, leaving 645 people unaccounted for. It is reasonable to assume that most of these individuals would have been of Portuguese origin. Statistics Canada's ethnic group data were based on a survey of one third of residents. Inaccuracies are possible; it should be noted that town officials and members of the Portuguese community usually gave higher estimates. For the census tract information, see Statistics Canada, *1971 Census of Canada - Census Tract Bulletin (Toronto), Population and Housing Characteristics by Census Tracts*, p. 43.

idents in 1972, included a large parade in honour of Our Lady of Good Voyage. The event drew spectators and participants from well beyond Streetsville.

In 1973, Portuguese Canadians were just beginning to enter the Streetsville retail scene as merchants. One of the first establishments, "Joe's Fish Market," was praised by the newly formed association representing downtown merchants for adding "something cosmopolitan" to the town. Burt Johnston, owner of the nearby Streetsville IGA, who stood to lose a small part of his business to the new store, sent flowers to the owners.[19]

The Streetsville Citizens' Organization for Retention and Expansion (SCORE), set up in 1972 to demonstrate to the province Streetsville's opposition to amalgamation, included the active participation of some members of the Portuguese community. Norm Pontes, for example, was a key member of the executive. Nevertheless, in 1973, few Portuguese-Canadian residents were part of the town's official civic leadership, including the committees, boards, and commissions. This can be partly attributed to the fact that language barriers still existed. Moreover, Simoes remembers that some immigrants were at least initially reluctant to get involved in public affairs because they were more accustomed to a system where political life was significantly curtailed,[20] as it was in Portugal during the long administration of Prime Minister Antonio Salazar.

The names of the local minor-league athletes were still almost exclusively Anglo-Saxon, although the Portuguese community organized the very popular Miramar Soccer Club. The club rented the basement of a downtown building, which it used as a social gathering place, especially for young adults.[21]

Streetsville had several churches in 1973, all of which were very active in the community. The places of worship included St. Andrew's Presbyterian Church, St. Joseph's Roman Catholic

Church (which had a weekly Mass in Portuguese celebrated by Father Kea), Streetsville Baptist Church, Streetsville United Church, and Trinity Anglican Church (where the mayor and her family were parishioners).

POLITICS AND ADMINISTRATION

The mayor of Streetsville in 1973 was the popular Hazel McCallion. She was raised in Quebec's Gaspé region, where she was born on Valentine's Day, 1921. She spent time in Quebec City and Montreal before moving to Toronto as a young adult. Leadership interested the energetic and athletic Hazel Journeaux at an early age. She was, for example, the first woman to serve as president of the Anglican Young People's Association of Canada.

In September 1951, she married Samuel Robert McCallion, a photographer who was born and raised in Mount Dennis (now part of the City of Toronto). That December, the couple moved to a home on the Britannia Sideroad (which was then merely a dirt road), just outside Streetsville. At the time, the future mayor was working in an office-management capacity with the Canadian Kellogg Company, where she spent a total of 19 years.

Hazel and Sam McCallion quickly became active in their new community. They opened a dry-cleaning business (Elite Cleaners) and a printing company (Unique Printing). Hazel McCallion was also a Girl Guide leader, eventually becoming a division commander. In September 1964, with the future mayor serving as president of the chamber of commerce, she and her husband founded the *Streetsville Booster,* the successor to their *Streetsville Shopping News.* The stated *raison d'être* of the new monthly tabloid newspaper was implied in its name—to promote Streetsville and its businesses. (Initially, no advertisements were accepted from outside Streetsville and the surrounding district.[22]) The McCallions juggled these responsibilities with the duties of raising a young family. When the *Booster* was established, the youngest of their three children, Paul, had only seen his first birthday.

In the fall of 1965, McCallion resigned from her chamber of commerce position to seek election as deputy reeve of Streetsville. It was a hotly contested election in a community with a history of competitive electioneering, not to mention a relatively high rate of voter participation in local elections. To be nominated, candidates did not simply turn up at the municipal offices with the requisite papers. Instead, a lively meeting was held, usually on a weekday evening, which the municipal clerk chaired (and often dreaded). Citizens interested in nominating their fellow residents, in being nominated themselves, or simply wishing to observe the spectacle unfold, would present themselves at the appointed public venue—usually a school gymnasium. Nominees would have 24 hours to decline a nomination. If nominated for more than one position, they would be required to indicate for which, if any, office they wished to let their names stand.

McCallion had a high profile going into that election. Under her leadership, the chamber of commerce had successfully urged town council to call a plebiscite on whether to permit liquor to be sold on licensed premises. The voters obliged by favouring an end to Streetsville's "dry" status. Shortly before the election, McCallion wrote that "even with amalgamation in the wind we will need a strong representation to ensure the best possible deal for Streetsville."[23] The election did not, however, end in triumph for her—she collected 625 votes, falling 200 short of her opponent, George Parker, a long-time municipal politician and a superintendent of the local Reid Milling operation.

McCallion was not deterred, however. A year prior to that election, she had been appointed to the Streetsville Planning Board. She had become increasingly critical of the board for simply dealing with issues as they arose, rather than working from an overall vision for the community and following a long-term critical path. Before long, her colleagues on the board installed her as the chair.[24]

Prior to the next municipal election in December 1967, McCallion put her name forward again for deputy reeve. This time she was successful, enjoying a comfortable margin over her new opponent, Councillor Ross Machin. She ran on a "Planning for People" platform.

McCallion told the author that she decided to seek public office because she was concerned that Streetsville "was run by a very tight group that controlled everything."[25] Many of the town fathers (they were all men before McCallion's election) were genuinely public spirited, but it is arguably true that they had not all fully grasped the exigencies of governing a modern municipality. Policy-making could be very *ad-hoc* and sometimes disorganized. There was limited strategic planning and an inadequate inventory of the town's assets.

McCallion's political fortune was reinforced in July 1968 when the reeve, Don Hewson, resigned because of his intensifying professional commitments. Within several weeks, the council named McCallion as Hewson's successor. An explanation is warranted here: After 1962, the reeve was not the most senior elected official in the community. When Streetsville's status changed that year from village to town, a mayor was added. The mayor, reeve, and deputy reeve were elected at large. They were joined by six councillors, two for each of three wards.

The mayor in 1968-69 was John J. (Jack) Graham, Q.C., a lawyer who worked in Etobicoke. Graham, a native of Cobalt, Ontario, moved to Streetsville in 1956, a year after beginning work specializing in family law. He was Streetsville's reeve in 1966-67, and also served as warden of Peel County in 1966—the last Streetsville resident to do so. Graham had been widely regarded as an intelligent and capable official. Even Hazel McCallion had thought so; her editorials in the *Booster* had frequently portrayed him as the one shining light on the 1966-67 council. The two were clearly allies in the December 1967 election campaign. "Wherever you saw one's sign on a pole, you saw the other's sign on a pole," recalls former reeve Hewson.[26] In late 1967, Graham shepherded through council several important downtown development-control measures which McCallion had worked on at the planning board.[27]

His Worship's term as mayor was a difficult one, however. Within several months of taking office, Graham was consistently at odds with McCallion. By March 1968, he was expressing dissatisfaction with the work of the two general committees, chaired by the reeve and deputy reeve.[28] He soon faced opposition to his urgent request to deed the property on which the public utilities commission building was standing to the commission itself for one dollar.[29] A complicated dispute over a boundary fence involving the Streetsville Lawn Bowling Club (whose green was owned by the town) and neighbouring resident J.A. Howson Brocklebank (himself a lawn bowler) took on a life of its own, becoming particularly messy and heated.[30]

Another stormy incident occurred in January 1969. The *County of Peel Act* required that two of Streetsville's top three elected officials serve also as county councillors, one of whom had to be the reeve. At the time, Deputy Reeve Bill Arch, a past county warden, joined McCallion at county council and proved to be a staunch ally of the outspoken reeve. But Mayor Graham was determined to return to county council, claiming a mandate from town council to explain Streetsville's recently released *Boundary Study*. At a January town council meeting, Arch was unceremoniously relieved of his county duties. He was not present at the time, and the recorded vote showed that only McCallion and Councillor Norm Thomas voted in his favour.[31]

A furious Arch submitted a letter announcing his resignation from Streetsville council. A few weeks later, however, he reported to council that, upon reflection, he intended to withdraw his decision—

an unusual but acceptable move, according to town solicitor Ward Allen, because council had not yet met to formally receive the letter. All told, however, Graham's handling of the matter created division. One Mississauga newspaper called his actions "ungentlemanly,"[32] although Arch—a World War I veteran, rags-to-riches businessman, and home-builder (known locally as "Danny" or "Little Danny")—was himself no stranger to controversy.

John J. (Jack) Graham, Q.C., warden of Peel County, 1966; and mayor of Streetsville, 1968-9. *Photograph courtesy of the Streetsville Historical Society.*

Intra-council politics were not Graham's only headache during this period. He had come to the view that radical municipal restructuring was necessary and that Streetsville had to be included—even if this meant amalgamation with the Town of Mississauga.* He was one of the few municipal politicians anywhere to speak approvingly of the provincially com-

---

* As late as the spring of 1965, Graham was still onside with the majority of town council, whose position he summarized as follows: "[A]malgamation so long as we are surrounded by agricultural lands almost wholly unserviced is premature and would create more problems than it would solve." ("The Reeve Reports," *Booster*, May 4, 1965.) But a year later, he was much more convinced that there should be a municipal merger as soon as possible: "When one considers the magnitude of the task of providing the basic services of communication, transportation, pollution control, recreational and institutional needs for a population this size [the 250,000 people expected to move into the West Credit area within the next 20-30 years], it becomes increasingly apparent that small municipal councils operating in restricted geographical areas ... clearly lack the capacity to do the job." ("The Warden Speaks," *Booster*, June 7, 1966.)

missioned *Plunkett Report* (1966), which would have effected a major
overhaul of municipal boundaries, including the disappearance of
Streetsville as an incorporated entity. At that time, Graham's views
had either been accepted or overlooked by most Streetsville residents,
perhaps because his one-time council colleagues who had spoken
most vociferously against the Plunkett-envisioned reforms were also
those who—rightly or wrongly—faced the most doubts about their
ability to govern the municipality. The Streetsville Ratepayers' Association, led by Robert Weylie (who would go on to be an outspoken
opponent of amalgamation as Streetsville's reeve in 1972 and 1973),
came out in favour of the *Plunkett Report* shortly after it was
released.[33] Even Hazel McCallion, as a member of the county's Committee on Regional Government in 1968, was initially charging that
the *Plunkett Report* was being rejected more by politicians than the
public[34]—a view which Graham had expressed while serving as the
county warden in 1966. At a joint meeting of Streetsville council and
the town's committees, boards, and commissions, a motion was
passed (supported by McCallion and Graham) requesting that
county council "consider a single tier system of Regional Government save and except for Hydro and water."[35] A county report
proposing the retention (at least for the time being) of the lower-tier
municipalities, while establishing the county as a regional municipality with new responsibilities for capital financing, sewers, water,
police, planning, and parks, was rejected by Streetsville on the
grounds that it did not go far enough.[36]

But by the end of the 1960s, the mood had obviously
changed. Several possible explanations can be offered: the reforms
of the 1968-69 administration may have convinced many residents that Streetsville could be an effective self-governing municipality; the highly publicized 1968 *Boundary Study*, which Graham himself had been instrumental in commissioning (although
he was much more skeptical of the results than were most of his

colleagues on council), prescribed territorial expansion for Streetsville, not amalgamation with Mississauga; the reform era (discussed later) had dawned in Streetsville and was casting the Mississauga politicians in a less-favourable light; and outspoken politicians like Hazel McCallion took up the cause of implementing the *Boundary Study* and of having the matter aired fully in public.* By the summer of 1969, Graham reported that even his seven-year-old daughter was being ostracized by her classmates over the question of Streetsville's survival as a town. He decided that he would not stand for re-election.[37]

This was McCallion's chance. With vigour, she threw herself into the race for the town's top position. She faced one opponent, Bill Tolton, who had been Streetsville's mayor in 1966 and 1967, before being defeated by Graham. Tolton, who had a degree in agricultural science, was a printer/publisher by occupation. Many of his views on local governance had long been progressive,† but his mayoralty had been a difficult one. In 1966, council had approved a tax

---

* The *Boundary Study* appears to represent a crucial turning point in McCallion's thinking on restructuring. She vigorously defended the document, and wanted to ensure that it, along with "Goals Plan II" of the Metropolitan Toronto and Region Transportation Study, which proposed "corridor cities" of which Greater Streetsville was one, would receive as much public exposure as possible. This position was clearly articulated in the November 27, 1968, report of Streetsville council's "Regional Committee," which McCallion chaired. The *Boundary Study* was endorsed by council on December 16, 1968. (Minutes, Region of Peel Archives, 1994.063, Box 3.)

† In a 1965 article, for instance, Tolton showed himself to be ahead of his time: "In Holland, for example, we find complexes of medium to high rise apartment building[s,] shopping centres and office buildings, and even larger factories, all designed as a unit, so that a worker can walk, in a few minutes, from his home to his work and do his shopping on the way. There is much to be said for this conception of living especially when these large-scale developments include parks, recreation centres and even little private

increase of 9.6 mills. Tolton was also being blamed for a simultaneous increase in councillors' honoraria from $360 to $750, and a rise in the mayor's stipend from $1,000 to $2,000, even though these increases had been approved the previous year, before the election. Tolton was also taking considerable flak for a bylaw to place modest restrictions on water use, although this move had been preceded by a long period of hot, dry weather, and despite the fact that the mayor was actively engaged in discussions with the province and the other southern and central Peel municipalities to bring in water from Lake Ontario. (The eventual outcome, launched in 1968, was the South Peel Water and Sewage Scheme, which involved an $88-million provincial investment over several years.[38])

Meanwhile, the Tolton council became entangled in controversy with the Streetsville Lawn Bowling Club and the Streetsville Public Library Board over the town's plans to begin construction of a new library building on the site of the old one.[39] This project had been authorized by the voters in a plebiscite. The new library would also take up the adjacent bowling green, which the club had been leasing from the town since the beginning of the century. Attempts to relocate the club fell through when the separate school board expropriated the appointed site. The lawn bowlers then argued that they had a right to occupy the original location, and that this was in fact stipulated in the terms by which the property had been deeded to the municipality by the Cunningham

gardens for those living in nearby apartments who have an interest in such things. And the cows still peacefully graze in an adjoining field.

"How much more realistic, efficient and economic in the use of land and resources such a concept is than the piecemeal urban sprawl that we have seen in the past few years, where thousands of acres of excellent farmland have become wastes of weeds. Rows and rows of houses have proliferated over our countryside creating all kinds of problems, calling for costly solutions in water, sewage, roads, schools." ("Planning, People and Progress," *Booster*, September 7, 1965.)

family in 1902. Tolton, who contributed considerable personal time and money to the library project, looked for another place to put the new building. His opponents charged that he negotiated a land-swapping deal without council's authorization in order to secure the new site (beside Centre Plaza).* Looking back, however, most Streetsville residents would probably concede that this was a fortunate sequence of events because the historic old library building was saved, and the still-in-use lawn bowl-

William Tolton, mayor of Streetsville, 1966-7. *Photograph courtesy of the Streetsville Historical Society.*

ing green, which is easily visible from Queen Street, functions as a quaint gateway to the historic downtown. Indeed, even the library board, which came out strongly in favour of building on the existing (lawn bowling) site, had itself prepared a report in 1965 which identified obvious disadvantages with that location, including the lack of public parking, the fact that it was not centrally located, and that the library would not be able to offer service during the construction period.[40]

McCallion came across in the 1969 mayoral campaign as dynamic, outspoken, and energetic. She took 826 votes to Tolton's 660. She was re-elected two years later, decisively defeating another former mayor, George Wilson. Going into 1973, which would turn out to be the last year of Streetsville's life as a municipality, McCallion said her New Year's resolution was to make "the West Credit

---

* McCallion's *Streetsville Booster* often led the charge on the library issue. The *Mississauga News* took a different view, accusing the *Booster* of presenting an exaggerated version of events. (See "Put up or shut up," *News*, June 14, 1967.)

Hazel McCallion, deputy reeve of Streetsville, 1968; reeve, 1968-69; and mayor, 1970-73. *Photograph courtesy of the Streetsville Historical Society.*

area a people's place rather than a developers' heaven."[41]

The influence and authority which McCallion obviously wielded in the office of mayor did not spring from her official, mandated powers. Ontario's municipalities had—and have—a "weak-mayor" system. The head of council has only one vote, no power of veto, and generally no additional formal mechanisms to craft policy beyond what others on council enjoy. The combined effect of the absence of political parties and the fact that there are fixed, rather than fluid, terms of office (meaning that there is no risk that a vote of censure or a policy impasse would trigger fresh elections, as in a Westminster-style system of cabinet responsibility) makes it especially difficult for a mayor to consistently control a block of seats on council. Although mayors are elected at large—and can, therefore, claim to speak for the whole municipality rather than only one of its wards—Streetsville's reeve and deputy reeve were also elected at large.

In such a system, mayoral influence comes from a populist instinct, public approval, effective persuasion, the ability to articulate a vision for the future, sustained energy, personal dynamism, a good grasp of the matters at hand, the tendency of the media to look first to the head of council for comment, the election of members of council with similar priorities, attentive groups and citizens willing to work with the mayor, and an issue or set of issues which galvanize politicians and the public. These ingredients appear to have been in place for Hazel McCallion. She had an air of authority, but did not come across as an elitist. She had an impressive capacity for hard work and long hours. She was also already displaying an asset which has been critical to her enormous popularity during her long career in public office—the ability not only to feel the public pulse but to come across as the people's principled champion. In a somewhat similar vein, political scientist James MacGregor Burns argues that successful leadership "is, in large part, [the ability] to make conscious what lies unconscious among followers."[42]

McCallion's populist qualifications have arguably included a penchant for zeroing in on ideas, initiatives, and individuals likely to help meet her or her constituents' objectives. In a 1965 article in the *Booster*, the future mayor foreshadowed her approach to politics:

> A generation or two ago it was said of two prominent business partners that one of them had a hundred impractical ideas in his head and one good one, while his senior partner had the experience and the mature judgement that enabled him to reject the hundred impractical ideas, to grasp the possibility in the good one and to apply it in their business. This rare combination of talent and practical common sense worked out happily for both and for all their customers and associates.
>
> If government today could find comparable talents among its leaders and could combine them in the same wholesome co-operation it might be able to convert the confusion that now prevails in parliament into orderly progress.[43]

It appears that throughout her political career, McCallion has endeavoured to operate in a manner resembling that senior partner. Whenever she is asked to identify public figures whom she most admires, McCallion names Charlotte Whitton (1896–1975). Whitton had a distinguished career as a child-welfare reformer and was later the feisty, strong-willed, and extremely hard-working mayor of Ottawa. Whitton's biographers have described her as "a feminist on the right."[44] McCallion, like her heroine, has often employed a crusading, decisive style. Although consistently an outspoken advocate for change and innovation, her political philosophy has also included a respect for traditional institutions such as the monarchy and a belief that voluntary community initiatives are often preferable to efforts by the state to achieve the same ends.

McCallion, who turned 52 in 1973, was among the oldest members on her town's governing body. She was joined on the 1972-74 Streetsville council (which, because of amalgamation, only fulfilled the first two years of that mandate) by Reeve Robert Weylie, who had defeated incumbent Bill Appleton in the December 1971 election. The deputy reeve, James S. Graham (no relation to the former mayor), also took an active interest in many files—including environmental issues, local marketing and identity, and organizing community celebrations.

The nine members of council met at 327 Queen Street South. Outside, a Victorian-style sign, adorned during the warmer months by a well-kept floral arrangement, announced that this was the "Town of Streetsville Municipal Offices [and] Police Department." Although constructed in 1858, the building had been a town office only since 1966. It was originally the Streetsville Grammar School and later the Streetsville High School, but ceased to be used for school purposes in 1951, when students were bused to either Port Credit or Brampton. (The $1.5-million Streetsville High School on Joymar Drive opened in 1958.) The municipal council had formerly held its meetings in the town core in the Streetsville Public Utilities Commission building.

The late Frank Dowling, who served on Streetsville village council between 1948 and 1961, and as mayor on Streetsville town council in 1962, recalled that preserving the former

The town council of Streetsville in 1973. Seated (left to right): Reeve Robert Weylie, Mayor Hazel McCallion, Deputy Reeve James S. Graham. Standing (left to right): Councillors Frederick Dineley, Edward Rea, Douglas Spencer, James Watkins, Graydon Petty, and Frederick Kingsford. *Photograph courtesy of James Graham. Photograph taken by A.W. Betts.*

school—which required the town to purchase it from the school board—was not a simple matter. "There were some people who wanted to tear the building down [and] they had formed a little pressure club," he told me in 1997. "Eventually, after some debate and disagreement, we put it to a vote and won. And that is how that building was saved."[45]

The structure was not much larger than many single-family homes which now dot the landscape around Streetsville. It had 3,047 square feet of useable office space and 1,300 square feet of basement storage room. The edifice is presently the city-owned Streetsville Kinsmen Senior Citizens' Centre.

Members of council were considered part-timers and were paid accordingly—even after the 1966 increase. A report filed with the province in 1971 shows that the mayor took home $2,500 per annum. The reeve, deputy reeve, and councillors each received $1,500.[46]

There was, of course, a staff of full-time and part-time employees who carried out council's wishes, tendered advice to the politicians, and attended to the day-to-day affairs of the municipality. The most recognized (and most senior) was Leonard McGillivary, who had been appointed clerk in 1953. He was referred to by the town employees and residents as simply "McGill." Since 1955, he had also served as a justice of the peace for Peel County, and he was a member of Streetsville's volunteer fire department. McGillivary, who died in 1995, came to Streetsville as a teenager, and his first job in town was with Canadian Pacific. He had no post-secondary education but achieved a great deal through hard work, recalls his wife, Winifred.[47] He had an occasionally gruff personality but also a heart which matched his large, imposing physique. "He always expected the best, but he also knew that there was a human factor," says Linda Evans, who was appointed as his secretary in 1970.[48]

Len McGillivary worked under a succession of elected officials, who varied considerably in their personalities and grasp of the issues. He managed to maintain cordial relations with most of them. Doug Spencer, a Ward 1 Streetsville councillor in 1973, remembers that McGillivary always seemed to sense how most deliberations would turn out.[49] He is also reputed to have known the *Municipal Act* like the back of his hand.

For most of the 1960s, McGillivary was the clerk-treasurer of Streetsville, but a separate treasurer's position was created in 1972 and he was thereafter designated as the clerk-administrator. At any given time in 1973, the town had between 25 and 30 employees.

The treasurer in 1973 was Emmaleen Sabourin, an Etobicoke resident who had spent six years as vice president of finance for Airwick Industries. That year—which would prove to be an exceptionally busy one for her—she was working on her AMCT (Association of Municipal Clerks and Treasurers) certification from Queen's University.[50] Although she had joined the municipal staff just a year earlier, she had already acquired a reputation for being very thorough and for knowing where every dollar went. The town's expenditures in 1972 amounted to $1,397,066—approximately $7,000 more than the previous year. This included $539,828 collected for education purposes (over which the town had no control, as these funds were simply turned over to the school boards) and $95,428 for the county levy. The town's greatest single expenditure category over which it had jurisdiction was "Protection to persons and property," totalling $168,010. Revenues added up to $1,394,052, almost 90 percent of which came from property taxes. Reserves had increased from $46,000 to $257,000 since 1971.[51] The mill rate was down 1.86 mills in 1972 over 1971 (translating into a $65 decrease for the average homeowner) and remained the same in 1973.[52]

Keith Cowan was Streetsville's director of public works. The functions he oversaw included the construction of roads, removal of snow and ice, and the maintenance of municipal equipment. Widely regarded as a consummate professional, Cowan brought considerable technical and engineering expertise to the position. A graduate in civil engineering from Queen's University in 1950, he had previously worked for the cities of Belleville and Ottawa. He was more qualified for his post than were his predecessors; before his appointment, many public works functions had been handled much less systematically, sometimes to the consternation of local residents.

The Peel Regional Police Service had not yet been established in 1973. Streetsville was served by its own 10-person force, headed by Donald Fletcher, who had commenced his career with the Fredericton City Police in 1955. He moved to Toronto a few years later and hoped to join the then-recently established Metropolitan Toronto Police. However, he noticed an advertisement for a constable's position in Streetsville, and he arranged to meet with Clerk McGillivary. That very evening, he was brought before council and his appointment was approved. By 1964, at the age of 27, he was chief of police, the youngest in Ontario. His deputy chief was Ted Rutledge, a well-known and respected resident.

All members of the force were at least reasonably well trained, having attended the Ontario Police College and having taken prerequisite courses in criminal investigation. "The term 'community-based policing' has since been coined," Fletcher says. "You see, we had just that; we just took that for granted. As soon as we amalgamated and became a regional force, that just disappeared. That was where we had the advantage. If something happened in Streetsville back in the '60s or early '70s we almost [always] knew where it was. We could almost put our finger on the suspect right away.

"No, we didn't have a bomb squad, we didn't have a morality bureau, we didn't have a homicide squad, but neither did a lot of the other small forces. They weren't needed."[53]

"If you had a problem in your store … [the Streetsville Police] were on the scene within minutes," confirms long-time local merchant and downtown property owner Eric Ladner. "Sometimes the cruiser was within a block of our store. If you had a break-in, no matter how minor it was, they were interested enough to come [quickly] to investigate it. In many cases they caught the people."[54]

"In those days, every officer on the force, right down to the last man, did a lot of volunteer work," Fletcher remembers. "We were really involved with the youth of the community." A "Policemen's Ball" was held every winter to raise money for local minor-league sports.

The former chief recalls, however, that there were changes by the early 1970s. More transients were coming through, and Peel's population was growing rapidly. "It was getting to the point, with the explosion of development around here, that a small police force would not be able to keep up with the influx of major crime." Streetsville's municipal status aside, Fletcher believed that an amal-

The Streetsville Police Department in 1973. Seated (left to right): Sergeant Jack Hunter, Chief Donald E. Fletcher, Councillor Edward Rea (chair of the Police Committee), Secretary Georginna Cooper, Councillor Douglas Spencer, Deputy Chief Edward Rutledge, Sergeant Robert Clarke. Standing (left to right): Constables Aubrey Gibson, Indrek Kahro, Dennis Wright, Robert Smythe, and Robert Walker. *Photograph courtesy of the Streetsville Historical Society.*

gamated—preferably regional—police force would eventually be formed. "It is coming soon," he told the *Mississauga News* in 1972. "And I think it's a great idea."[55]

The crime rate was low in Streetsville, but there were some incidents. In November 1972, a typical month, the Streetsville Police Department served 68 summonses, 13 warrants, answered 319 complaints, and responded to five fire or bank alarms. There was one auto theft, six other thefts, one assault, and one break-and-enter.[56] Several similar incidents made the local papers in 1973. In addition, there were a number of serious traffic accidents which required attention, a few of them fatal. That year, the Streetsville Police, along with other emergency services, even responded to the crash of a small airplane on the grounds of the Chrysler plant, just outside the town's boundaries.

The Streetsville constables would occasionally assist the appropriate personnel in ensuring that the town's bylaws were being observed. Dogs had to be annually licensed at a fee of five dollars, or three dollars if the renewal was done before February 15. New Year's Day, 1973, also marked the start of bicycle licensing, at an annual charge of one dollar; officials had apparently become concerned about the number of lost or stolen bicycles. Wooden fences could not be higher than six feet, and barbed wire was banned outright. All swimming pools required a building permit. Overnight parking was prohibited on town streets.[57]

The police station at the town hall was one of the places where the alarm would sound whenever there was an incident requiring the prompt attention of the fire department. There were no full-time firefighters; this was the Streetsville Volunteer Fire Department. Members received a small honorarium from the town, the most going to Chief Kirby Burns who earned $250.

"It was a good, satisfying job," remembers Dave Spear, who joined the department in 1968. "It was a way of putting something back into the community." Another former member, Andy Viens, recalls that the firefighters received regular training and had to follow a strict schedule. There were set times when they could not leave the community for any reason.[58]

Although Streetsville's firefighters were not full-time, the department had come a long way since its humble beginnings. In the early days, bucket brigades would be assembled using the wells and pumps of local citizens, says Burns. But in 1937, the department was reorganized under Chief Lenvard Lee. Two years later, it got its first motorized firefighting apparatus, a 350-gallon GMC Bickle Pumper, which is still brought out for some local events.

Lee, a funeral home director, resigned in 1949 to run for village council. After Lee's successful campaign, Burns, who had served with the Corps of Canadian Firefighters in Britain during World War II, assumed charge of the department. "One thing I learned overseas is that you don't go out without equipment," he recalls. He never abandoned this principle as chief.

In December 1972, Mayor Hazel McCallion handed Chief Kirby Burns the keys to the town's new fire truck. The ceremony took place during the firefighters' popular annual Santa Claus festivities. *Photograph courtesy of Kirby Burns.*

By the time Streetsville celebrated its centennial in 1959, it had a new fire station at the corner of Broadway and Tannery Streets, and its fire department was described as among the best volunteer brigades in the province. *Through a Century with Streetsville*, a book issued to commemorate the municipality's anniversary, explained that one reason for the department's success was its practice of regularly upgrading and adding equipment: "Some of the newest additions to the fire department's equipment are the latest type of electronic resuscitator, inhalator, smoke ejector and breathing apparatus," the publication boasted.[59]

Burns's position at the helm of the fire department was secure in 1973, despite some hip problems. He was highly regarded for his competence and professionalism. When the Streetsville Citizen of the Year Award was established in 1960, he was its first recipient. "He has often been referred to as a true gentleman and that is what he was," remarks Gord Bentley, the deputy chief in 1973. Dave Spear concurs: "You could not have worked for a better man. He was, and still is, the most diplomatic man you could ever meet."

Burns led a contingent of 18 men in 1973. Also under his command was an impressive new vehicle—a Thibault-Ford quint with a 100-foot aerial ladder. (The truck left Streetsville after amalgamation to serve central and southern Mississauga.) There were some serious, even tragic, incidents which required the fire department's prompt and efficient response. The last major call of 1973 turned out to be a fatal fire: on Boxing Day morning, a boiler exploded and completely gutted a home on John Street, claiming the life of a visitor from White Rock, British Columbia.[60] A community fund was immediately set up to help the suddenly homeless family of Maria and Emanuel Santos.

The firefighters were very active in the community in other ways. They enthusiastically supported muscular dystrophy research. Every December, they would drive Santa Claus (a.k.a. Vic Johnston) up and down Queen Street in a fire truck and would later hand out gifts to the hundreds of local children who came to the fire hall. Santa would then proceed to the local nursing home to bring Christmas cheer to the residents.

The town had a municipally run daycare centre, under the direction of Karen Midwinter who was assisted by four teachers and a cook. The facility opened on September 18, 1972. Located in a new building in Gatineau Park in the north part of the town, the centre, which could accommodate 45 children in the two- to five-years age group, featured modern indoor and outdoor play areas. A citizens' group, the Day Care Centre Advisory Board, met regularly to review the operations. René Brunelle, Ontario's minister of community and social services, announced at the opening ceremonies that Streetsville's was the 880th licensed daycare facility in Ontario.[61]

THE BOARDS AND COMMISSIONS

Not all public officials who provided local services in Streetsville reported to the town council; there were several semi-autonomous boards and commissions. Many local-government experts have been extremely critical of such "fragmentation," arguing that it compromises accountability and prevents elected officials from effectively defining priorities and formulating broad, coherent public policies. An oft-cited poetic criticism of special-purpose bodies first appeared in Professor Henry Mayo's *Niagara Region Local Government Review*, 1966:

> The councillors up at Pitlochry
> Believed in the creed of ad hockery
> They farmed all decisions
> To Boards and Commissions
> And so made their council a MOCKERY. [62]

But governance in the Town of Streetsville was not a mockery. Experienced, capable citizens were given the opportunity to share their expertise without imposing a financial burden on the municipality (the members of these boards and commissions were paid a token honorarium, or nothing at all)—an important consideration where the tax base is limited. Although the ability to hold identifiable, elected politicians (rather than more obscure, single-purpose commissions) accountable for policy outcomes is important in a healthy democracy, a vibrant community also requires meaningful citizen participation. These boards and commissions provided concrete avenues for residents to take ownership over their local affairs.*

---

* Alexis de Tocqueville, the brilliant 19th-century French traveller and political thinker, observed that widely distributing local decision-making responsibilities could contribute greatly to educating and inspiring citizens, as well as constructively channelling their ambitions and acquainting them with the nuances and dilemmas of public life. Tocqueville, *Democracy in America*, Harvey Mansfield edition (Chicago: University of Chicago Press, 2000); see, for example, p. 64.

Streetsville's head librarian served under the Streetsville Public Library Board, which was chaired by Ian Ferguson, a local resident who was then the principal of Erindale Secondary School in Mississauga. With the exception of one councillor (Fred Dineley), the board consisted of non-politicians appointed by council.

There had been a library in town since 1854, when it was part of the Farmers' and Mechanics' Institute. The library operated out of the former Cunningham Tinsmith Shop (now known as the "Streetsville Village Hall") from 1902 to 1967, when the controversial 6,500-square-foot Centennial Library at 127 Queen Street South was opened.

Librarian Elizabeth Colley, appointed in 1971, was the first person with formal library training to work for the board. Colley, born in Calgary, served with the Women's Royal Canadian Navy Services before graduating with a BA in History, English, and Philosophy and working for a secretarial agency in London, England. Colley returned to Canada in 1966, and in 1969, at age 55, she completed her degree in library services. She worked in Brampton before coming to Streetsville. The historical society's Mary Manning, herself a former Streetsville librarian, lauded Colley as "a newcomer [to Streetsville] who was passionately interested in the village and eager to add to the local history collection." (Indeed, Colley delighted the society when she was able to find a copy of the 1895 Street family genealogy through a Boston antiquarian bookdealer.)[63]

The library was open five days a week (it was closed Wednesdays and Sundays) from 1 p.m. to 9 p.m., except on Saturdays when it maintained the hours 10 a.m. to 5 p.m. The Juvenile Department kept different hours on weekdays: 2 p.m. to 5 p.m. and 7 p.m. to 9 p.m. The library had a book stock of slightly more than 20,000, and at the end of 1972 a total of 4,357 people had library cards. Streetsville was part of an inter-library loan system,

The controversial Streetsville Public Library building was constructed in 1967 as a Centennial project to replace a smaller facility. *Photograph courtesy of the Ruth Konrad Collection of Canadiana, Mississauga Central Library.*

which in 1972 satisfied 469 requests for books owned by libraries throughout the country.[64]

"The library was a real meeting place. It was very community oriented," Colley remembers. She explains that the board ran "a very tight ship" and carefully reviewed every expense. The library, nevertheless, offered many different activities, including children's story times, craft lessons, and educational lectures.[65] At a board meeting in early 1973, Mayor McCallion exclaimed that she had heard "nothing but glowing comments concerning the Library Board and the librarian."[66]

Water and hydro in Streetsville were overseen by the Streetsville Public Utilities Commission. Streetsville remained outside the Ontario Hydro family until 1934, when the PUC was finally established following a local plebiscite. The municipality had already constructed a dam in 1906, at a cost of $20,000. The system was managed from the late 1920s until the late 1950s by the "legendary" John Temple, who has been described as the "one man who kept the village electric power and water supply operating with scarcely ever an interruption."[67]

Since the late 1960s, the water came from Lake Ontario (not the Credit River or local wells). It was supplied to the PUC by the Ontario Water Resources Commission and later the Ministry of the Environment. The necessary infrastructure (the South Peel Water and Sewage System) had been largely paid for by the province, and was put in place to service the actual and anticipated growth in the Town of Brampton and the Township of Chinguacousy, as well as Streetsville.[68] Indeed, the system allowed growth to accelerate.[69]

By all accounts, Streetsville's PUC operated well. The commission's manager in 1973, John Wiersma, was a professional engineer and a graduate in electrical engineering from McMaster University. "The system was being expanded rapidly," he remembers. "It was a time of change."[70] There were about 1,800 customers in 1973.[71]

The elected commissioners received no remuneration, and this would usually make any complainants less antagonistic, recalls Ron Walker, the PUC chairman in 1973. Walker and his colleagues were consistently re-elected, and power and water rates did not arouse too much consternation. In a June 1972 press release to mark Hydro Month, the PUC boasted that,

> Service and reliability has [sic] greatly increased. One item that has been relative to other costs and practically constant, is the cost of power to the consumer. Your Public Utilities Commission has endeavoured to keep rates to a minimum. Electricity is still a bargain when you consider that for 1 cent you can operate the average: Steam iron—45 minutes; Kettle (Electric)—35 minutes; 2 slice toaster—40 minutes; College Study Lamp—4 hours.[72]

The commission was an efficient operation, Walker remarks. "If the lights went out, the manager might be up a pole within a few minutes." There were only six-and-a-half full-time-equivalent employees. "Later [after amalgamation] there was better equipment, but the crews wouldn't get there that quickly."[73]

The planning board made recommendations to council about local development and land-use issues, and a parks and recreation board* did the same about matters within its purview, although both had some authority to enact their own bylaws.[74] Under the parks and recreation board's jurisdiction was Memorial Park, a 28-acre site which included a lighted softball diamond, two soccer fields (one regulation size, one junior), picnic tables, children's playground equipment, a splash pool, sandbox, bleachers, and parking spaces. A hill on the west side of the park was often used in winter for tobogganing. Other parks included Markborough Park (7 acres), Gatineau Park (15 acres), and Riverview Park (20 acres).[75]

Also situated in Memorial Park was Streetsville's outdoor swimming pool (40 feet by 85 feet), which had opened in 1966. Modest user fees were charged.[76] In a 1971 plebiscite, a majority of voters cast ballots against the construction of an indoor pool.

The parks and recreation board could always count on Vic Johnston, one of the community's most active citizens (often referred to as "Mr. Parks"), to devote considerable time to the upkeep of its facilities. "He was very philanthropically inclined, a dedicated resident," recalls Ralph Hunter, who chaired the board in 1973. Johnston, who had moved to Streetsville from Shelburne in 1928, had also served for more than three decades on the Streetsville Public Utilities Commission and was probably its most knowledgeable member. He was 79 years old in 1973. He suffered a stroke that January, which kept him away from his duties for

---

* In 1972, town council merged the parks board and the recreation committee.

more than three months. But by the spring, no one could stop him from resuming most of his activities.

"He was extremely prudent about spending money, almost to the point of not spending it," Hunter remarks. "Vic was a very stubborn person; [but] he was stubborn to the benefit of the parks and recreation. If he felt that someone was abusing the system, he would get his heels dug in and he would almost override democracy. He just made it happen. Even if the [board] had said, 'No, Vic, we have to do it this way,' Vic would say 'Okay'. You would come a week later and it was done exactly the way he wanted it, not the way we wanted. But it was always the right way."[77]

Next to the pool was the Streetsville Arena, which was officially named after Vic Johnston on June 25, 1973. It was a separate non-profit corporation. The facility, completed in 1961 at a cost of $250,000, had not been built with tax dollars but with citizens' donations and the hard work of local groups—especially the Lions Club. The board of directors employed two full-time maintenance officials. The complex's operations were supported by ice and floor rentals, concessions such as skate sharpening and a snack bar, as well as the rental of the 45-foot by 90-foot community hall. The board's policy was that local activities should take precedence over out-of-town organizations for the always-in-demand ice time.[78]

THE BUSINESS SCENE

Streetsville's business community was reasonably robust, although deliberations about the future of the downtown (discussed in Chapter 5) were making it clear that the commercial/retail sector would need to change. Some of the industrial outfits in town were Reid Milling (flour), Dominion Sash (sash and door manufacturers), C.T.S. of Canada (electronic control manufacturing), Tube Benders and Fabricators Ltd. (metal fabricating), Wilcox Auto Bodies (truck and auto body manufacturing), and Derby Pet Food Ltd. (which sponsored the Streetsville Derbys). Just outside Streetsville's munici-pal limits was the massive Chrysler manufacturing plant (an 805,000-square-foot building which was officially opened in September 1972), as well as McCarthy Milling (flour), F.B. McFarren Ltd. (brick manufacturers), and Canada Brick. The Streetsville area was producing about 10 percent of Canada's flour.

Some of the older industries experienced difficulties. In April 1971, for example, the Quaker Oats plant closed. In a newspaper interview, Jack Graham, the outspoken former mayor, was not afraid to weigh in with his concerns: "It's the council of Streetsville," he argued. "They don't get public support from the merchants. They get it from the subdivisions. These are people who live in Streetsville and work in Toronto. They just want a nice quiet place that's away from the noise and growth. If they want something like that they should move 100 miles north of North Bay to get it." Town council countered that there was no basis to these accusations, and argued that proactive measures were being taken to attract business and industry to the town.[79]

Nevertheless, commercial and industrial assessment as a pro-portion of overall assessment was rather low (a little more than one fifth), probably partly as a result of Streetsville's limited land base—something which council was trying to ameliorate by advo-cating for an expanded territory for Streetsville. The commer-cial/industrial portion had been decreasing since 1966, when it stood at 30.5 percent. The largest decrease happened between 1968 and 1969, when commercial/industrial fell from 27.5 per-cent to 23.6 percent of overall assessment.[80]

Although the Erin Mills and Meadowvale developments had important ramifications for Streetsville, and although the develop-ment issue figured prominently in the amalgamation debate, the developers were not major players or even assertive lobbyists in town; most of their investments were situated in the Town of Mississauga.

As late as June 1969, Streetsville's council and planning board were observing that the town had almost no role in the discussions on the major land developments. Streetsville officials planned to attend a special meeting in Mississauga to ask whether the developers would "consider changing the phasing of the development to start their development outwards from the Town of Streetsville." They also wished to enquire if the companies' executives had reviewed the town's *Boundary Study*.[81] Soon after, Streetsville established a "Development Liaison Committee," chaired by Hazel McCallion. Although the town never fundamentally opposed development, it remained somewhat distant from—and suspicious of—the builders' grand promises and flamboyant styles.

LAND DEVELOPMENT AND THE REFORM MOVEMENT

Streetsville was not oblivious to the sprawl which was almost at its doorstep, but dealing with these new pressures could be difficult. In 1967, the planning board hosted a large meeting at Streetsville Secondary School to discuss future land use in the community, particularly in the downtown core. The subject proved controversial, even emotional. There was a feeling that the town was being threatened by formless, monolithic development—not only on its periphery but in the core itself. Some historic buildings had already been demolished, and others were threatened. Shortly thereafter, a temporary development freeze was approved to allow the civic leaders to get control of the situation and carefully plan for the future. Although the freeze had long since expired by 1973, the town was still very cautious.

In late 1972, Mayor McCallion issued an important and widely publicized policy statement on the future of Streetsville. The 11 major objectives which she articulated were as follows:

1. The acquisition of approximately 500 acres of land along the east and west side of the Credit to be used for open space in the area from the proposed 403 to 401.

2. A pedestrian walk-way ... along the east bank of the Credit with the necessary footpath bridges being built over the Credit to connect to the west side.

3. To officially declare our policy of acquiring land along the Mullett Creek to bring about a continuous open space along both sides of the Mullett Creek. Pedestrian footbridges at specific points to connect those open spaces on both sides of the Mullett Creek.

4. A major overhaul of our Official Plan with a careful review of the densities contained therein at the present time and with the viewpoint in mind of reducing the amount of high density to a minimum. This town is known as a low density urban area and our policies and objectives should be to retain it as such. This applies to both vacant land and especially land for redevelopment.

5. To re-evaluate our Commercial zoned land and more clearly define our Commercial areas to make it a more dynamic Commercial Core.

6. Preservation of Historical buildings by processing the necessary By-laws to accomplish same and at the same time preparing architectural control By-laws which will govern any redevelopment in the downtown core. This will also set guidelines for the Municipality in providing the necessary services in the downtown core.

7. A vigorous continuation of our plan to eliminate overhead services (poles and wires) from our downtown core and continue throughout the community.

8. Implementation of an internal and external transportation system with the viewpoint ... of being prepared for the Magnetic Levitation Transportation System just unveiled by the Provincial Government.

9. The location of a major recreational complex to serve as a sports centre to ensure that our valuable parkland will remain as open space.

10. Restoration of the Millraces on the Credit and other traditions that formed such a vital part of this area's past, with a view to re-establishing the Historical and Pioneer traditions of the Town of Streetsville.

11. An intermediate plan for the housing of the Municipal and Administrative staff with a long term objective of a Civic Centre within the area.[82]

This statement is significant for several reasons. Many of these policies clearly looked well beyond the boundaries of the existing Town of Streetsville. The town could not, for example, simply proceed to acquire all the aforementioned natural areas between Highway 401 and (the still-to-be-constructed) Highway 403, because much of this land was within the Town of Mississauga.

To account for such discrepancies, one must again take note of the *Boundary Study* commissioned by the town in 1968. As is discussed in more detail in the next chapter, the document's key recommendation was that Streetsville apply to annex almost 10,000 acres of the surrounding lands, an area several times larger than the existing municipality.

The policies in the mayoral statement largely reflected the temper of the times. A certain restlessness was in the air, not only in Streetsville but in other centres (especially urban communities). In Toronto, for example, reformers such as John Sewell—who took pride in being "up against city hall" even after being elected to council[83]—were sweeping away the old guard, which had come to be identified with big money, big developers, and insensitivity to ordinary residents.

Although often channelled into vigorous citizens' movements, the reform ethos was generally rather conservative. In a 1970 article,

Toronto reform councillor William Kilbourn described himself as a "tory radical." He explained it thus: "It is to be radical in the rejection of the ugliness that dominates so much of our community in the name of progress. It is to be tory in a commitment to the good values and amenities of the past which are being eroded away."[84]

Toryism and social activism are not polar opposites or necessarily incompatible. Indeed, the Canadian tory tradition is, in many ways, distinctly at odds with the rugged individualism, glorification of the free market, and contempt for public institutions exhibited by many neo-conservatives. Canadians who have been influenced by a tory philosophy have, by and large, been advocates for moderation and critics of excess of all kinds, be it in government *or* the private sector. Generally speaking, tories favour gradual, not cataclysmic, change. They believe that there is such a thing as the "common good" and that collective interests as well as a healthy respect for tradition must sometimes take precedence over individual wants and ambitions. Although tories are often concerned about the consequences of big government and large bureaucracies, social consciousness and concern for the less fortunate are usually readily discernible in the tory analysis of public policy.*

Of course, political ideas are not fixed. They sometimes change in response to particular circumstances, generational replacement,

---

* Prominent Canadians who have been identified as espousing a tory philosophy include Stephen Leacock, George Grant, Eugene Forsey, Robert Stanfield, and David Crombie. For an excellent review of the political thought of several tories, see Charles Taylor, *Radical Tories: The Conservative Tradition in Canada* (Toronto: House of Anansi Press, 1982). The British political figure often regarded as a source of inspiration by conservatives is Edmund Burke (1729-1797). As Conor Cruise O'Brien persuasively demonstrates, Burke was not a narrow-minded reactionary. His parliamentary activities and writings were almost always directed against excess and extremism in all its forms. Burke was thus entirely consistent in passionately rejecting the French revolution and equally passionately

and demographic factors, among other causes. Nor is it always possible to place an individual into a neatly defined ideological category; the real world is, after all, a complex place. A case in point is the evolution of the Streetsville mayor's policies and priorities. In the same speech in which her 11 policy objectives were presented to the public, Hazel McCallion exclaimed that "it has been the record of this community to support plans which put 'people first' and development second."[85] Actually, several years earlier a local politician would have been less likely to make the distinction. Development would have been seen as good in itself, especially by elected officials who always had one eye on local assessment—the more development you can attract, the better the chance you can hold the line on taxes (at least in the short term) for existing ratepayers (that is, voters), and (presumably) more business will be generated for the merchants. In a 1966 *Booster* editorial, McCallion (who was not yet in elected office) had herself opined that:

> There seems to be a great need for housing in our Town, on both a purchase or rental basis. It also seems to be the opinion of many, especially the merchants, that we need more people in Streetsville. The big question then is: WHAT or WHO is holding up the development of the land owned by Markborough Properties Limited within the Town of Streetsville?[86]

One should not conclude that Streetsville and its mayor had become radically anti-growth by the early 1970s; indeed, McCallion still sometimes spoke positively of Markborough, and the town hall was by no means bolted shut to the developers.[87] But with the reform movement in ascendancy, few would have disputed the wisdom of holding up a development proposal to ensure that it com-

___

denouncing the corruption and cruelty of the British administration in India. See *The Great Melody: A Thematic Biography and Commented Anthology of Edmund Burke* (Chicago: University of Chicago Press, 1992).

plied with public objectives that had come to be defined more broadly than short-term economic infusions.

Of the 10 local councils in Peel County, the reformist disposition was most evident on Streetsville's. Already during Jack Graham's mayoralty, there was a distinct move toward careful and coordinated planning, greater public participation, preservation of green space, political transparency, professional and predictable administration, as well as careful scrutiny of development. The 1968-69 council moved speedily (often spurred on by Hazel McCallion) to change the way the town was run. Council decided that before it issued any building permits, input would be sought from the public utilities commission, the school boards, the parks board, the recreation committee, the planning board, the fire department, and the police department. All written resolutions before council would be decided by recorded votes; the press or the public could find out how each member voted—there would be no hiding on controversial questions. Mechanisms were put in place to encourage more youth input.[88]

When McCallion took the mayor's gavel in 1970, she was accompanied by several others who had joined her in espousing a reform agenda on the previous council— including Bob Weylie, Jim Graham, and Bill Appleton (although the latter, who came to support amalgamation while the others became strong opponents, eventually found himself out of favour with most of his council colleagues and ended up losing the following election). After the next election, in late 1971, council consistently displayed unity on most of the key issues.

Completely surrounding Streetsville was the Town of Mississauga. It had a land area about 60 times larger than Streetsville's, and its population was approaching 200,000 in 1973. Mississauga grew by 10 percent that year,[89] although most of the development was still concentrated in the town's southern half. Mayor Robert

Speck and his successor, Charles "Chic" Murray, who took the reins after Speck's death in April 1972, had more in common with Toronto's William Dennison than they did with Streetsville's Hazel McCallion. When, for instance, Mississauga's chief engineer urged council to require flamboyant and influential developer Bruce McLaughlin to help install sewers in a new subdivision prior to road-building, rather than leaving the town to do it later at greater expense, Mayor Speck snapped, "If we want to build a city, which I think we intend to do, then putting these restrictions on McLaughlin would break him before he got started."[90]

Streetsville was sharply critical of the way Mississauga did business. McCallion accused Mississauga and the developers of "attempting to create instant cities with instant history." This, she insisted, proved that, "To retain [Streetsville's] identity we must remain a municipal entity."[91]

Increasingly, however, the Mississauga politicians were hearing criticism from within. The local newspapers, traditionally promoters of rapid development, were once full of praise for the "foresight" of the Mississauga politicians in forging a "well-managed town."[92] The developer-designed Erin Mills and Meadowvale "new towns" had been trumpeted as "exciting and modern" showcases of an "environmental atmosphere."[93] Meanwhile, in 1970, the *Mississauga Times* had condemned Streetsville for "a ludicrous and parochial attitude towards a space-age technology [by which was meant massive, modern, suburban developments] it cannot comprehend."[94] Within a few years, however, the *Times* had clearly departed from its earlier boosterism. Even the *News*, although almost always strongly pro-developer, was somewhat more subdued. Alarm bells were ringing about faulty or inadequate planning, as well as lax enforcement of building standards. The *Times*, in an editorial on July 5, 1972, observed that, "The signs of consumer discontent with the building industry are many.... Both the province and the town must seek to restore balance and competitiveness to the industry. Otherwise, Mississauga's building boom is a bust."[95] By the end of the year, the same newspaper was also opining that "the developers who have struck gold because of Mississauga's too-fast development should be expected to pave the streets with some of that gold."[96] Although the *Times* did not explicitly take Streetsville's side in the amalgamation battle, its 1973 editorials portrayed the town as progressive, professional, and public-spirited.

The public grumbling in Mississauga was perhaps not as audible as in Toronto, where Mayor Dennison's political woes had become acute by the time he retired at the end of 1972. The city's old guard was being accused in many quarters of displaying what internationally renowned scholar Marshall McLuhan (who had a hand in local activism in Toronto) denounced as a distinct lack of "interest in the values of neighbourhood or community."[97] Nevertheless, many Mississauga residents were beginning to say the same thing about their town. Martin Dobkin, a young physician, knew this, just as he knew that the public desire for change in Streetsville was not confined to that municipality. The sun had not set on 1972 before Dobkin had convinced himself that Murray could be beaten, and that even he, although relatively unknown, could topple him.

In part because of the philosophical differences between the civic leaders in Mississauga and Streetsville, and in part because of the deep disagreements over local government restructuring, the relationship between the two municipalities, at least at the political level, was downright chilly after 1970. Almost every publicly discussed issue in which these towns had an interest turned into a feud. Two prominent controversies of the early 1970s were a railway crossing over the proposed Erin Mills Parkway, which would be a county road just west of Streetsville

(Streetsville argued for a bridge or tunnel because of the anticipated heavy traffic, while Mississauga was satisfied with a level
crossing for the time being) and municipal servicing of the huge
new Chrysler plant, just north of Streetsville. "The town of Mississauga has the responsibility for putting [industry] there and
Streetsville has the responsibility for solving the problems," a
frustrated McCallion told the *Globe and Mail* in 1972.[98]

*   *   *

As Streetsville entered 1973, the year in which its future as a
municipality would be decided, it could reflect with satisfaction
on the fact that it was a vibrant community, with an exciting, par-
ticipatory civic life. It could also look with some unease and trep-
idation at the storm clouds that loomed.

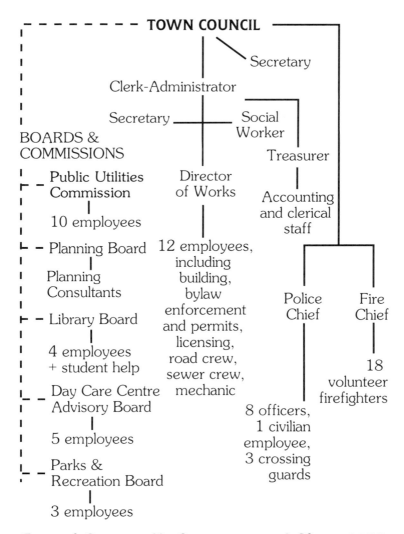

TOWN COUNCIL

Secretary

Clerk-Administrator

Secretary — Social Worker

Treasurer

BOARDS & COMMISSIONS

Public Utilities Commission

10 employees

Director of Works

Accounting and clerical staff

Planning Board

12 employees, including building, bylaw enforcement and permits, licensing, road crew, sewer crew, mechanic

Planning Consultants

Library Board

4 employees + student help

Day Care Centre Advisory Board

5 employees

Parks & Recreation Board

3 employees

Police Chief

8 officers, 1 civilian employee, 3 crossing guards

Fire Chief

18 volunteer firefighters

Town of Streetsville Organizational Chart, 1973

TOWN OF STREETSVILLE
BOARDS AND COMMISSIONS, 1973

STREETSVILLE PLANNING BOARD

Victor C. Dale	J.R. McLeod
D. Brian Morris	Gordon K. Yetman
Gloria Goodings	Orval A. Johnston
Trevor Redmayne	Mayor Hazel McCallion
Reeve Robert M. Weylie	Councillor D. Graydon Petty

STREETSVILLE PUBLIC UTILITIES COMMISSION

R.K. Walker	Dan M. Richmond
Victor C. Johnston	Unitt C. Bailey
Mayor Hazel McCallion	

COMMITTEE OF ADJUSTMENT

W.S. Sharpe	A.C. Randles
David Y. Lewis	

STREETSVILLE PUBLIC LIBRARY BOARD

Ian Ferguson	Hugh Manning
Beryl Walker	Mary Dobson
Councillor Frederick Dineley	

STREETSVILLE PARKS AND RECREATION BOARD

Ralph Hunter   Hugh McPherson
Victor C. Johnston   Councillor Edward P. Rea
Councillor Frederick S. Kingsford
Trustee Norah Busby (Peel County Board of Education)

DAY CARE CENTRE ADVISORY BOARD

Margaret Black   Helen McIsaac
Joan Laurie   Sandra Emerson
F. Robert Estey   Chester Rundle
Joan Brandrick   Councillor James L. Watkins
Councillor Douglas D. Spencer

The Regional Government Question

2

On the evening of January 23, 1973, several hundred people gathered at Hamilton's Mohawk College. Most of the seats were filled well in advance of the arrival of John White, the minister of the treasury, economics and intergovernmental affairs, and one of his parliamentary assistants, York East MPP Arthur Meen.*

It was Meen who had the unenviable task of presenting the provincial government's proposals for municipal restructuring in the area west of Metropolitan Toronto, affecting the counties of Peel, Halton, and Wentworth, as well as the City of Hamilton.

---

* There was no Ministry of Municipal Affairs in 1973. Instead, most of the functions formerly overseen by that ministry were contained within two of the seven divisions of a "super-ministry"—Treasury, Economics and Intergovernmental Affairs. The super-ministers, including John White, usually had more than one parliamentary assistant.

A few weeks before the announcement, the government was careful to point out that the proposals would not be cast in stone. This time, nevertheless, there was a sense that the announcement would be a crucial one. Government statements in 1972 appeared to make it clear that Queen's Park would finally proceed with changes.

Several regional governments had already been established by that time: Ottawa-Carleton (1969), Niagara (1970), Muskoka (1971), York (1971), Waterloo (1973), and Sudbury (1973). In each case, simultaneous consolidations of lower-tier municipalities took place.

Streetsville's political contingent at the gathering was led by Mayor Hazel McCallion. She had been apprized of the main points in advance, and she was not amused. Even before Meen appeared at the podium, McCallion was vigorously denouncing the proposals in interviews with the media.[1]

The short document which was made public at that raucous session proposed that the 10 municipalities in Peel County be amalgamated into three, within a new Regional Municipality of Peel. The towns of Streetsville and Port Credit would merge with most of Mississauga and a small part of Oakville.

McCallion's displeasure was augmented by what was unveiled for Halton County. Its seven municipalities were to be reduced to four, despite that county council's recommendation that there be three. Milton's insistence that it form an additional lower-tier municipality with expanded borders was acceded to. Streetsville perceived a double standard.

The proposal also outlined the anticipated division of powers between the new regional municipalities and the lower-tier units (referred to as "area municipalities"). The regions would assume more powers than the counties had: there would be new planning responsibilities, policing, and water, to name a few key areas. The Streetsville politicians did not preoccupy themselves excessively with these points. By far the single most important concern to them was that Streetsville would be submerged into a much larger city.

The *Toronto Star*'s Ian Urquhart charged the next day that Streetsville's mayor opposed the scheme because she did not want to lose her job.[2] A *Globe and Mail* editorial on January 26 criticized McCallion for wanting her "pie left as it was."[3] Such analyses were simply inadequate; amalgamation debates had raged for many years, and there were more than knee-jerk reactions at play. This chapter reviews the sequence of events and discussions which preceded the provincial announcement of January 1973.

THE EVOLUTION OF MUNICIPAL GOVERNMENT

In 1792, Lieutenant Governor John Graves Simcoe divided Upper Canada into counties for militia purposes and to serve as electoral districts for the new colonial assembly. By the early 19th century, townships were being surveyed, with often straight and arbitrary boundaries. A few more decades would pass, however, before the townships and counties became genuine units of local government.[4]

Colonial officials were initially very reluctant to create elected municipal governments. Partly because of the perceived restlessness and instability of the United States, democracy was a tainted concept among the ruling elite. (The personal interests and profits of the Family Compact were almost certainly also a factor.) Times were changing, however, and by the mid-1840s moderate reformers were in control of the assembly and cabinet of the Province of Canada. (Upper Canada and Lower Canada had become one colony in 1840.) The comprehensive *Municipal (Baldwin) Act*, which received Royal Assent in 1849, provided for some local autonomy.

Townships and counties (Peel became a separate county in 1867) were not the only units of local administration. Various clustered settlements had taken shape outside the original main towns. The people of these communities developed collective interests and wished to provide for common needs, which often differed from those of the nearby rural residents. Many of these communities asked to be designated as separate villages or towns. Streetsville's incorporation as a village in 1858 was part of this pattern of separating town and country.

The Confederation arrangement made it clear that, constitutionally, municipalities were wholly subordinate to the provinces (section 92 of the *British North America Act*). And the provinces have flexed their jurisdictional muscles—increasingly so as more complex, modern problems emerged. It has thus been common for municipalities to be called "creatures of the provinces."

In the 1960s, Stefan Dupré described the provincial-municipal relationship as "hyper-fractionalized quasi subordination." This phrase—although "barbarous," as Dupré himself conceded—illustrates the complexity of the relationship; many ministries and a plethora of local institutions are involved. The subordination is "quasi," not total, in part because municipal politicians are elected and therefore command some legitimacy. The province has often deemed it prudent to exercise a degree of caution.[5]

Notwithstanding the complexity of the provincial-municipal relationship, there has often been in Canada a fixation with local government boundaries. Amalgamations (and, in an earlier era, the carving out of new municipalities) have often been held up as magic solutions to all manner of local problems. By contrast, in the United States—where state governments have often tied themselves down with instruments like "Home Rule" charters—there have been few forced municipal consolidations since the massive New York merger of 1898.[6]

In considering boundaries and municipal consolidations, one must have a view of the purpose of local government. A statement in the *Report of the Royal Commission on Local Government in England* (1969) is as appropriate and succinct as any:

Local government is not to be seen merely as a provider of services. If that were all, it would be right to consider whether some of the services could not be more efficiently provided by other means. The importance of local government lies in the fact that it is the means by which people provide services for themselves [and] can take an active and constructive part in the business of government....[7]

How this applies to municipal consolidation depends on where one puts the emphasis. If one regards as paramount the need for citizens to "take an active and constructive part in the business of government," a small-scale administration might be desirable. On the other hand, for a local polity to actually provide services for itself, or to have the clout to arrange services according to its priorities, a somewhat larger population and land base could be more appropriate.

GROWTH AND CHANGE IN PEEL

Peel's agricultural sector remained very strong until after World War II. Population growth was minimal and the county was largely rural. But things were to change dramatically.

The post-war baby boom, economic growth, Toronto's urban sprawl, significant immigration, and rapid technological advancement (these phenomena were at least somewhat intertwined) suddenly wrested the county from its slumber. Many parts of southern and central Peel began to experience major population growth. New suburban neighbourhoods were sprouting in fields where wheat and corn had grown.

The expansion was not without its growing pains. In Toronto Township, which completely surrounded Streetsville (and which had boundaries that were roughly similar to those of today's Mississauga, minus Port Credit and Streetsville), the haphazard development and lack of political assertiveness in planning ahead for sufficient amenities and infrastructure resulted in steep property tax increases in the late 1940s and early 1950s. The frustration of Toronto Township residents led to the election of Professor Anthony Adamson, and then Mary Fix, to the office of reeve. Fix, a highly educated and urbane lawyer, spearheaded a policy of better-planned growth, which included attracting new business enterprises to ease the burden on the residential ratepayers.[8]

Fix also broke new ground by issuing a forceful call for the amalgamation of Toronto Township with Streetsville and Port Credit, or at least the creation of a "metropolitan administration"* for the urbanizing parts of Peel.[9] She believed that such a move would pre-empt any attempts to bring the township into the recently formed Metropolitan Toronto, which was chaired by the savvy and highly influential Frederick Gardiner.

Fix did not have much time to promote her plan. She was defeated at the polls in late 1959 by Robert Speck, a councillor, farmer, and businessman. Although he was less visionary than Fix, Speck was outgoing and energetic. He continued to press for amalgamation or a metropolitan set-up for the southern half of Peel. This concept received a cool reception from the other municipalities that would have been affected by such restructuring, and Speck was sometimes mockingly referred to as "Little Daddy", a play on Gardiner's "Big Daddy" nickname.[10] Meanwhile, a county-commissioned financial study by the firm Glendinning, Campbell, Jarrett and Dever advised that amalgamation or a new metropolitan structure would be expensive, complicated, and that any advantages could easily be realized through inter-municipal agreements.[11]

Ever-conscious of the perceived Metro threat, Toronto Township politicians were also actively contemplating applying for city

---

* This term was used before "regional government" became the expression of choice in the mid to late 1960s. The regional government blueprints did, after all, take their inspiration from the Metropolitan Toronto model.

status*—with or without Streetsville and Port Credit—as well as changing the municipality's name. The reasons were manifold, but it should be noted that Streetsville had annexed some land from the township several times in the 1950s and 1960s. It was thought that upgrading the township's status (to a town or city) would put the brakes on such incursions. Finally, in 1968, Toronto Township was made a town—without Streetsville and Port Credit. In a plebiscite, its voters chose the name "Mississauga" over "Sheridan."

THE PROVINCE STEPS IN

The province had to come to terms with the new demands associated with the post-war growth around Toronto. The creation of the municipality of Metropolitan Toronto was, in part, a response to this. A rather weak regional planning authority was also instituted for Metro Toronto and environs (including Streetsville).

Realizing that these efforts were not sufficient, the government of John P. Robarts launched, in 1962, the Metropolitan Toronto and Area Transportation Study (MTARTS) to propose how public and private vehicular traffic could be managed and accommodated in the future. Jurisdictional and boundary issues were also being pushed to the fore by many analysts and pundits, who argued that government units created in the 19th century were not adequately or rationally structured to meet the challenges of the latter part of the 20th century. Accordingly, while MTARTS was in progress, the province approached Thomas J. Plunkett, a respected expert in municipal affairs who was also a lecturer at McGill University and a past city manager of Buckingham, Quebec. Plunkett's mandate was to come up with recommendations for local-government restructuring in Peel and Halton.

---

* City status would have also meant separation from the county.

Concluding that "a fundamental reorganization of municipal government in the area is imperative,"[12] Plunkett proposed that the Township of Toronto and the towns of Streetsville, Port Credit, Brampton, Oakville, Milton, Burlington, and the portion of the Township of Chinguacousy that was under development by Bramalea Limited be amalgamated to form a single, one-tier municipality, which he referred to as the "Urban County of Mississauga." It would have a powerful mayor and 19 councillors.

Plunkett's report unleashed immediate criticism from municipal leaders, who argued strenuously that a local government covering such a vast area could not possibly work. If Plunkett's key recommendation had been implemented, the population of the "Urban County of Mississauga" would today be more than 1.2 million (and growing rapidly), spread over a very large territory. Even Municipal Affairs Minister Wilf Spooner quickly distanced himself from the recommendations, declaring that Plunkett "isn't Moses leading the Israelites and he isn't God."[13]

But the sweeping nature of Plunkett's vision lent credence to the notion that changing times required changes (even radical changes) to municipal boundaries. This was reinforced by the 1967 *Report of the Ontario Committee on Taxation* (the body was also known as the "Smith Committee" or "Smith Commission"), which argued that "in the interest of [enhancing] local autonomy, provincial responsibility for revision in municipal boundaries has become inescapable."[14]

Those who became advocates of comprehensive municipal restructuring, and in particular the creation of "regional governments," justified their positions by pointing to what they saw as the need to: improve community planning through integrated regional plans, rather than poorly co-ordinated municipal plans which encouraged the misuse of land to maximize short-term tax revenues; balance assessment-rich and assessment-poor areas to achieve a relative equality of services; and create stronger units of government below the provincial level, so as to mitigate the need for provincial micro-management of local affairs.[15]

The 1967 conclusions of MTARTS were received somewhat more favourably than the *Plunkett Report*. The transportation study team determined that it was difficult to propose strategies or solutions without knowing where further growth would be channelled. The authors, therefore, suggested their own alternatives. In two of the five possible growth patterns (especially "Goals Plan II"), Streetsville was featured as a regional or sub-regional centre, distinct from the Mississauga urban area.[16]

These scenarios were taken into consideration as part of the most important research effort ever undertaken by the Town of Streetsville—the $18,000 *Boundary Study* of 1968. Three consulting firms* were commissioned to jointly recommend appropriate, sustainable, long-term boundaries for the town. The growth in the counties near Metro Toronto had convinced Streetsville's council that the town could not remain the same—if it did, it would simply be swamped by development which it could not control.

Not surprisingly, the consultants concluded that Streetsville's geographical area should be greatly expanded, but they specifically asserted that there would be nothing to gain from amalgamating with Mississauga. The authors predicted that Streetsville's population with the new boundaries would reach 110,000 by the year 2000. (With the existing boundaries, the population could barely attain 12,000.) The area north of the future Highway 403, west of the Credit River, south of Highway 401, and east of the river's watershed limit (just beyond the Mississauga boundary with Oakville— the latter then occupied much of what is southern Milton today) would be within the new Streetsville.

---

* Municipal Planning Consultants Co. Ltd.; Glendinning, Jarrett, Gould & Co.; James F. MacLaren Limited

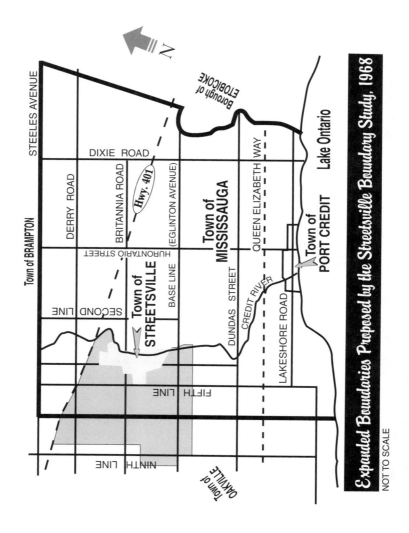

Expanded Boundaries Proposed by the Streetsville Boundary Study, 1968

NOT TO SCALE

The *Boundary Study* conceded that the town had managed to maintain a respectable balance sheet, despite ranking eighth out of 10 in the county in per capita assessment. The consultants argued, however, that expansion was critical to the community's long-term viability. "We have seen many examples of financial strangulation of a municipality where industry located outside its boundaries and demanded central urban type services from the town," they reported. "The results have been, to say the least, chaotic."[17]

The consultants proposed that a commercial/municipal centre be constructed using part of the area north of the future Highway 403 around the Base Line (now Eglinton Avenue), not far from where Erin Mills Town Centre is today. The old downtown would still be "a major local service area." Streetsville's official position in 1973, on the other hand, did not contemplate any plans to move the downtown far from the existing location. That submission envisioned an eastern municipal boundary well beyond the Credit River, thereby keeping the existing built-up area near the geographical centre of the expanded town.

In January 1969, shortly after the release of the *Boundary Study*, the minister of municipal affairs, W. Darcy McKeough, came forward with a tentative proposal for restructuring Peel and Halton. He wanted to join the two counties and create seven lower-tier municipalities out of the 17 which then existed. Streetsville (or a Greater Streetsville) would not have been among these municipalities.[18]

Hazel McCallion, who acquired the mayoral chain of office in January 1970, was advocating Streetsville's continuation as a municipal entity, with the expanded boundaries. She was telling anyone who would listen that "Streetsville is concerned about all the bad planning going on around it."[19] She had no choice but to hit the ground running. A few weeks after taking office, she was meeting with McKeough to express concern about his proposals.

Throughout 1969, McKeough was confidently vowing to move forward with his plan. As late as December 3, he advised the clerk of Mississauga that "I will attempt to have the discussions on regional government brought to a successful conclusion during 1970."[20] Meanwhile, he objected strongly to a county council motion calling for a Peel-only region, emphasizing that he was "deeply troubled by the limited scope and attitude evident in this resolution."[21]

But on March 9, 1970, the provincial government officially abandoned the 1969 proposals. In a subsequent speech to the Bolton Rotary Club, McKeough conceded that a consensus was lacking, but promised that one would continue to be sought.[22] The minister was also now insisting that it made more sense to first put forward an overall development plan for south-central Ontario, and then proceed with the structural reforms.

Streetsville's spirits were raised two months later when that plan was revealed. The maps accompanying *Design for Development: The Toronto-Centred Region,* based closely on Goals Plan II of MTARTS, showed Streetsville as a "service centre" distinctly apart from Mississauga. It would be surrounded by "parkway belts," which were to be set aside as corridors for green space, transportation, water and sewage facilities, and other needed infrastructure. These belts would also help to physically distinguish urban communities within the Greater Toronto Area, to prevent the whole area from becoming one sprawling, uninterrupted mass. Some media outlets interpreted the plan as prescribing a distinct "city" for the Streetsville area. It was likewise noted that Streetsville's *Boundary Study* was remarkably consistent with the new provincial announcement.[23] Not surprisingly, a town council resolution quickly affirmed "the whole-hearted support of the Town of Streetsville in implementing the plan."[24]

Despite the earlier suggestions that the *TCR* plan would

influence the redrawing of municipal boundaries, McKeough appears not to have changed his mind about Streetsville. Within a week of the announcement, Mississauga planning commissioner Henry Petschar told the *Toronto Star* that the minister had assured him there would be no annexation of Mississauga lands by Streetsville.[25] Before the month was out, even Hazel McCallion was saying that she was worried that pressure exerted by the developers would force the province to back down. Streetsville charged that the Metropolitan Toronto Planning Board—whose jurisdiction included Mississauga and Streetsville—appeared to be infringing on the future parkway belts* when it approved the plans for the Erin Mills community.[26] As well, in late 1970 and early 1971, Streetsville's politicians became concerned that Mississauga residents living in the immediate vicinity of the town were being told to use "Mississauga" in their addresses, rather than "Streetsville" as they always had. Postal services are, of course, a federal responsibility, but this did not stop McCallion from trying to enlist support from McKeough. The first draft of the minister's response (January 4, 1971) stated that, "Perhaps I could comment to the effect that there is little doubt in my mind that Streetsville as we know it will disappear as major local government reforms are established in the area."[27] The final version omitted this statement.

---

* In the ensuing few years, the province seemed hesitant about following through with the *TCR* vision, despite all the positive (and sometimes exaggerated) press headlines referring to plans for sophisticated transportation networks and a giant park between Hamilton and Cobourg. See, for example, *The Tail of the Elephant: A Guide to Regional Planning and Development in Southern Ontario* (Toronto: Pollution Probe, 1974). See also, Virginia Vito, Bureau of Municipal Research, "Erosion on the Parkway Belt?" (September 1973)—Archives of Ontario, RG 3-49, tb 38, Davis General Correspondence, 1973.

It was widely believed in Streetsville that the scuttling of the 1969 Halton-Peel proposals could be at least partly attributed to the area's representative in the legislative assembly, Bill Davis, an influential member of the cabinet of Progressive Conservative Premier John P. Robarts. Davis, a lifelong Conservative and native son of Brampton who frequently expressed pride in his small-town roots, had succeeded Colonel T.L. Kennedy as the member for Peel in 1959. (Following a redistribution, Davis represented the Peel North riding, which still included Streetsville.) In 1962, at age 33, he became the minister of education.

A file now at the Ontario Archives contains some fascinating, rough, handwritten commentaries on the internal political dynamics related to municipal restructuring in Peel. The author is unknown, although the file belonged to civil servant J. Gardner Church. The heading is "a la Dick Picherack." The latter was a senior research officer in the Ministry of Municipal Affairs at the time of McKeough's Halton-Peel proposals. These documents make reference to Davis's concerns: it is noted that he was "discontent" with the Halton-Peel scheme; that he "does not support" these ideas; and that "Kennedy [Doug, the member for Peel South] and Davis in Peel [were] afraid."[28]

Nevertheless, the reasons for the province's ambivalence and hesitation probably went beyond discussions between Davis and McKeough. It is clear that Premier Robarts was becoming concerned about the political ramifications of bringing in the new regional governments. The public was already showing signs of discomfort with the massive reforms to school boards (and the costs which seemed to be associated with that exercise). Many commentators were relating the regional government initiatives to a program of "rational" restructuring which was getting out of control.[29] Even former premier Leslie Frost warned Robarts to proceed slowly.[30] Although the Mississauga politicians seemed to favour the 1969 ministerial proposal, the other municipalities in the county were not at all receptive.[31]*

But McKeough was getting frustrated with the impasse. Just hours after he shelved the Halton-Peel proposal, Streetsville council passed a resolution to apply to the Ontario Municipal Board to annex almost 10,000 acres (7,000 from Mississauga and 3,000 from Oakville)—a measure consistent with the recommendations of the *Boundary Study*.[32] Streetsville's politicians insisted that the move was not far-fetched. Regional boards were running the schools, and the province was taking care of most of the cost of the South Peel Water and Sewage System, which meant that the new financial and administrative burdens resulting from the much-increased territory would not be overwhelming.[33] Although rapid growth was imminent, the area surrounding Streetsville was still sparsely populated and would immediately add just a few thousand residents to the town. The *Boundary Study* had itself spelled out how the transition could be smoothly carried out.

The Mississauga politicians were furious at this exercise. "Streetsville's annexation attempt is a deathbed repentance for lack of foresight by former town councils," alleged Councillor Lou Parsons.[34] Mississauga responded by applying to annex all of Streetsville. Meanwhile, Mississauga decided to step up its efforts for city status, which would mean separation from the county. Mississauga claimed that this move was in response to a county resolution supporting a Peel-only region with an expanded

---

* All sorts of theories were advanced to explain why the 1969 proposals had been abandoned. The *Globe and Mail*'s Dennis Anderson insisted on March 30, 1970 (in an article entitled "Trust is lacking between Mississauga and its neighbors"), that the tensions between Streetsville and Mississauga had much to do with it, although he did not cite any sources or offer concrete evidence.

Streetsville and Port Credit and a much-diminished Mississauga.[35]

In a letter to the Streetsville and District Chamber of Commerce, dated July 3, 1970, McKeough noted that "interim decisions" might have to be made with respect to the Streetsville and Mississauga applications.[36] Indeed, he actually contemplated letting the OMB deal with the cases, but he was strongly advised against it by the ministry's staff on the grounds that resolving such a major question at the quasi-judicial, appointed municipal board would be an abrogation of the government's responsibility for bringing in a comprehensive policy.[37] Three months before receiving this advice, an increasingly impatient McKeough had written to Davis, attaching the requests from Streetsville and Mississauga. "Perhaps you can advise me as to how I can reply to them," he told his cabinet colleague. "Seriously, Bill, we have to get on with this one way or the other."[38] In the end, however, none of these applications was heard by the OMB, and for the time being no decisions were made.

In 1971, a new municipal affairs minister, Dalton Bales, wasted little time before asking his deputy minister, Bill Palmer, for a briefing on the Streetsville situation. Palmer's document, prepared by the ministry's Local Government Organization Branch, summarized the issue thus:

> The basic problem which has to be resolved sooner or later is the issue of the status of the Streetsville area in the context of a future municipal structure for the area....

> The Department has not questioned the value of the growth concept embodied in the Streetsville Boundary Study. However, it has questioned the ability of a small municipality with limited resources to implement the plans. On the other hand, Mississauga is larger in population and has a good record in dealing with planning and rapid urban growth.[39]

The provincial civil servants would not diverge from this assessment,* despite the growing concern among residents of both Streetsville and Mississauga that the latter municipality's planning and administration were too responsive to the interests of developers. On the other hand, Streetsville, in the late 1960s and early 1970s, had been building what was widely perceived as an assertive and progressive political and administrative team.

In the midst of the relative peace which prevailed during the approximately one year Bales spent as minister of municipal affairs, the issues associated with regional government and amalgamation never went away for the Peel politicians. Streetsville continued to strategically position itself—reinforcing, for example, its support for a Peel-only region, which McCallion had called "the lesser of two evils" shortly after taking office.[40] "Peel has a fantastic history," council exclaimed in a short 1971 position paper. "It is known throughout Ontario as the 'Banner County.' There is a community spirit somewhat thin at times because of distance, but the spirit that exists in Peel is far greater than what would exist if Peel and Halton were put together as a region."[41]

This posturing had everything to do with Streetsville's desire to preserve its municipal status, albeit with expanded boundaries. If a Peel-only region were to be established, the lower-tier municipalities would be less likely to be amalgamated in the manner envisioned by McKeough's 1969 proposal. Having a Peel-only region with just three local municipalities would mean either giving the amalgamated South Peel municipality effective control

---

* McKeough had expressed similar views. In the aforementioned Bolton Rotary Club address of March 1970, he opined that, "A plan to dismember the successful municipality of Mississauga must bear in mind that this municipality has compiled an enviable wealth of experience in resolving the issues of rapid urban growth."

over regional council or limiting it to less than 50 percent of the seats—thereby permanently sacrificing the principle of representation by population. Streetsville obviously calculated that with a Peel-only region, South Peel might be broken up. Moreover, by favouring a Peel-only region, Streetsville could hope to generate support from the central and northern Peel municipalities, whose leaders were strongly opposed to the county joining Halton.

THE ELEVENTH HOUR APPROACHES

By late 1971, there were, again, very audible public rumblings. County council was about to embark on a study of reorganization options. Regional government schemes were still being implemented or announced in other parts of the province, and county politicians believed that Peel would not be left alone much longer.

The county's Municipal Organization Committee was directed to examine various options. Members argued at great length about several maps showing possible municipal boundaries within a future Peel Region. Hazel McCallion, who was on the committee, favoured "Plan F," which included a much-enlarged Streetsville with boundaries similar to those proposed by the 1968 *Boundary Study*. Early in the process, however, Streetsville sensed that the cards were stacked against it. There was, of course, no hope of Mississauga being on Streetsville's side. And although Streetsville cultivated alliances with some of the other Peel municipalities, the town was worried that an undesirable deal could be hatched among the majority of county councillors should Mississauga agree to a minority of seats on a Peel-only regional council (which would allow central and northern Peel to retain their influence) in exchange for the absorption of Streetsville and Port Credit. Several Streetsville resolutions and statements in 1972 therefore called on the province to come forward with a proposal without waiting for county council.[42]

When the Municipal Organization Committee voted in early spring 1972 to focus its research on "Plan C"—which included only three lower-tier municipalities, with Streetsville effectively swallowed by Mississauga—many Streetsville politicians and residents began pushing for a dramatic display of public opinion. The Streetsville Citizens' Organization for Retention and Expansion (always referred to as "SCORE"—hardly anyone remembers what the acronym stood for) was a huge effort. It was chaired by Blake Goodings, who also headed the South Peel chapter of the Association of Professional Engineers of Ontario. SCORE's petition collected 3,147 signatures, the majority of adult residents in Streetsville and the immediately surrounding area. The petition was translated into Portuguese, signs were printed, an essay contest was organized in local schools (the theme was "Streetsville—A Place to Stand, a Place to Grow," an expression taken from an upbeat song about Ontario often used on the Tory hustings),* motivational speakers such as Colin Vaughan of "Stop Spadina" fame met with residents, and a "drop-in centre" was opened at Queen and Pearl Streets.

The SCORE executive held a 90-minute meeting with Bill Davis, who was by then more than a year into his service as premier of the province. Goodings came away from that encounter encouraged; Davis, he believed, would not bring in regional government in Peel unless there was a clear consensus from county council, which was not yet forthcoming. However, in a subsequent letter to town

---

* One of the winners of the essay contest was George Carlson, the present councillor for Ward 6 (which includes Streetsville). Carlson was then a student at Dolphin Senior Public School. Part of his submission argued that the differences between Streetsville and Mississauga were symbolized by the two municipalities' welcome signs. Streetsville's, Carlson observed, were bright, colourful, and inviting, with well-tended little gardens. Mississauga's, on the other hand, were dull and dilapidated. The winning entries were reprinted in the *Booster*, May 2, 1972.

council, SCORE—no doubt realizing the dangers of relying too heavily on county council—maintained that the province should make a decision soon about Streetsville's never-abandoned application to annex lands from Mississauga and Oakville. By mid-May, SCORE decided to fade into the background, having made its point with the trappings of a full-fledged election campaign.[43]

Within a few months, the province was sending very clear signals that time was running out on the status quo. Darcy McKeough, who was back in charge of municipal affairs as part of a larger super-ministry, announced in June that the first priority for local government restructuring "will be to arrive at findings and recommendations for the reorganization of local government in the Toronto-Centred Region."[44] McKeough also asserted that Queen's Park was prepared to take the initiative: "[T]he province recognizes now that it is perhaps too much to ask of municipal politicians to be the authors of what is ultimately and properly provincial policy."[45] This contrasts somewhat with Davis's comments on a local radio program less than three weeks earlier, when the premier stated that the province would wait for a "degree of consensus" to emerge among the local leaders.[46]

McKeough does not recall Streetsville's lobbying making a strong impression on him. "I don't honestly think so," he says. "Hazel wasn't the power then that she is now—or has been for the last 20 years. She was mayor of a little town. She did not have much influence on Bill Davis, for example."[47]

However, for at least a few weeks in the summer of 1972, the possibility of an expanded Streetsville as part of a new regional government appears to have been contemplated by the provincial civil servants. In late June, McKeough asked the staff to present him with three options.[48] The alternatives which came forward a few weeks later can be summarized as follows:

- **Alternative I:** A Halton-Peel region, without Burlington (which would go to Hamilton-Wentworth) and also excluding

Caledon Township and about half of Albion Township (which would join Dufferin County).

- **Alternative II:** A Peel-only region with three area municipalities. This was essentially the "Option C" favoured by the county's Municipal Organization Committee, but it would have a 30-seat regional council with the majority of seats (16) going to South Peel (Mississauga).

- **Alternative III:** A Halton-Peel Region, including Burlington, but minus Caledon Township.

What is most significant for our purposes, however, is that Alternatives I and III included a "Streetsville," which would take in all the Mississauga lands north of Eglinton Avenue. This area's total population at the time was slightly less than 23,000.[49] The ministry bureaucrats had long favoured a Halton-Peel Region. Perhaps they assumed that including an expanded Streetsville would allow such a proposal to garner support from at least a few local politicians (namely Streetsville's) within the premier's constituency.

At some point between early July and August 16, 1972, the Streetsville option was dropped, as was the idea of excluding part of northern Peel. Because the original options were prepared for McKeough, it is likely the decision was his—although he would almost certainly have consulted with, if not taken direction from, Bill Davis. On August 16, the cabinet's Policy and Priorities Board was presented with a Halton-Peel option, with or without Burlington, as well as a Peel-only model with three area municipalities. Neither of these options contained a separate Streetsville. The Peel-only alternative was selected for further consideration,* despite the civil servants' cautionary note about the "serious political imbalance that

---

* In an interview with Brampton-based CHIC radio on June 2, 1972, Davis said that a Halton-Peel Region would be "unlikely." (Archives of Ontario, Clare Westcott recordings, F 2094-8-0-40.)

the present proposed two-tier structure would impose in Peel. A further option might be to establish a one-tier municipality with a ward system. In this latter approach, the inclusion of only that part of the county up to 17 Sideroad [Mayfield Road] or thereabouts should be considered."[50] It was also pointed out "that there has been no complete agreement on these boundary proposals. Streetsville and Port Credit in particular have objected. In addition, the northernmost municipalities are very concerned about the question of representation."[51]

Mississauga's Lou Parsons, the county warden that year and widely regarded as a close confidant of Bill Davis, took the hint that change was coming. He prepared a report and used his influence in late August and early September to get the county council—by a 12 to 10 vote and a 26 to 18 weighted majority*—to formally recommend "Plan C" to the province.[52] Mississauga, Streetsville, and Port Credit would form one municipality, while Brampton, Chinguacousy Township, and the Township of Toronto Gore would become a central Peel municipality. The remaining municipalities—Caledon, Albion, Bolton, and Caledon East—would be amalgamated. Some of the county councillors supported this proposal only very reluctantly.[53] Streetsville's representatives, Mayor Hazel McCallion and Reeve Robert Weylie, were among the chief opponents. McCallion dismissed the whole exercise, saying again that the province, and not the county, was responsible for municipal restructuring.[54]

The report that came before cabinet in December 1972 virtually ignored the Streetsville position.[55] Instead, much was made of Peel County's official position. By contrast, the proposals for

---

* Peel's county council had a complicated system of weighted voting, designed to give some recognition to the population factor (although it fell well short of this goal, especially by the 1970s). Streetsville's four votes were divided between Reeve Weylie and Mayor McCallion.

Premier William G. Davis delivers a speech at the January 1973 meeting of Peel county council, as outgoing warden Louis H. Parsons looks on. *Photograph courtesy of the Archives of Ontario (F 2094-7-1-57 #9A).*

Halton and Hamilton-Wentworth were careful to assess public and political opinions in Milton (which wanted to be a fourth area municipality within Halton, with expanded boundaries), Burlington (which did not wish to be part of Hamilton-Wentworth), and East Flamborough (which wished to be part of Hamilton-Wentworth).

As 1972 gave way to 1973, the residents of Streetsville were oblivious to these behind-the-scenes discussions. Many hoped that the outspoken front which their community had presented would persuade the provincial authorities that any new Peel Region should include a municipality centred on Streetsville.

COUNTY COUNCIL'S VOTE
ON WARDEN LOU PARSONS' 1972 REPORT
RECOMMENDING A PEEL-ONLY REGION
WITH THREE LOWER-TIER MUNICIPALITIES:

1. Mississauga-Streetsville-Port Credit;
2. Brampton-Toronto Gore-Chinguacousy;
3. Caledon-Albion-Bolton-Caledon East

Municipality	Number of Members	For	Against
Mississauga	5	5	
Streetsville	2		2
Port Credit	2		2
Albion	2		2
Caledon East	1	1	
Toronto Gore	1	1	
Bolton	2	2	
Brampton	3	1	2
Caledon	2		2
Chinguacousy	2	2	

3 Streetsville Fights Back

"Streetsville Mobilizes for Action!" declared the *Booster* following Streetsville council's deliberations on January 29, 1973.[1] For its part, the Mississauga press was predicting that Streetsville and Port Credit would mount a significant challenge to the just-released provincial proposal.

But Port Credit's forces did not materialize. Cy Saddington, an accountant and the mayor of the lakeshore town, was clearly dejected after the January 23 Mohawk College presentation. He at first promised to continue calling for a separate and expanded Port Credit. But the Port Credit front—if there ever was one—was soon to crack. Councillor Ed Donner was among the first to break ranks, announcing that a Port Credit ward on the new city council would be enough to placate him.[2]

The demoralized and divided nature of Port Credit's response was not surprising. Many citizens were very frustrated with the town's haphazard planning policies. Taxes were higher than in the other Peel municipalities, and in 1972 evidence surfaced that the council had knowingly borrowed beyond the municipality's means—an illegal action.[3] Perhaps most important, Port Credit had already long been surrounded by built-up Mississauga neighbourhoods.

Indeed, Saddington himself could not have been accused of being excessively optimistic about his town's life expectancy. In November 1972, the *Globe and Mail* had asked him and McCallion whether they thought that their respective municipalities would survive. Saddington's response was a rather pessimistic, "I have no idea." McCallion: "Definitely."[4] His Worship would eventually relent when his last-ditch attempt to salvage something—by urging that the new South Peel municipality be named Port Credit (and not Mississauga)—failed.

MISSISSAUGA HAPPY

Mississauga's politicians greeted the provincial announcement with expressions of satisfaction. "If we'd written it ourselves we couldn't have done it better," exclaimed Mayor Chic Murray.[5] A few days later, Murray somewhat more contemplatively lamented the loss of three important industries (Kraft, Canadian Tire, and Union Carbide) because the proposed boundary of South Peel would be drawn slightly south of Steeles Avenue.[6]

Overall, however, the mayor of Mississauga and his colleagues remained content. They had been given almost everything they had been seeking when they contributed to the Peel County brief in 1972. There would be only three municipalities in Peel, and Mississauga would remain virtually intact.

But the proposal left Mississauga at an undeniable disadvantage. The new city would be home to about two thirds of the residents in the region, but would be given only 46 percent of the seats on the new regional council. (This would prove to be a serious sore point for future city councils.) Even the provincial civil servants were concerned, as was indicated in various internal memoranda and reports.[7] The backgrounder distributed by the provincial government for the January 1974 inaugural meeting of the new city council praised the Town of Mississauga: "On its own initiative, the Town Council voluntarily and generously indicated that it was prepared to go into a regional system without a majority of representatives on the regional council. This unselfish act contributed a great deal to the acceptance of the new system by a majority of Peel County Council."[8]

Why did Mississauga agree to such a representation formula? Was the town willing to accept the plan because of anticipated savings to the taxpayers? This is unlikely. In an August 18, 1972, letter concerning a three-municipality, Peel-only regional model, which closely approximated the province's eventual course of action, Mississauga's elected officials actually predicted that the town's finances would be "affected adversely" (albeit "only very slightly").[9]

Ron Farrow, the civil servant who headed the province's Local Government Organization Branch in 1973, speculates that Mississauga might have simply recognized "the logic" of better-co-ordinated planning and municipal services.[10] However, the opposition parties at Queen's Park were not reluctant to ascribe more cynical motives to Mississauga's position. Mississauga, they claimed, was overjoyed that Streetsville would not take over part of its territory, especially the Erin Mills and Markborough developments. The Liberals and the New Democratic Party alleged that the Davis administration was more than happy to accede to Mississauga's position because of Queen's Park's own unhealthy association with the major development companies, which did not wish to be subjected to Streetsville's more demanding conditions for doing business.[11]

The records at the Archives of Ontario do not contain many pieces of correspondence on the regional government issue from land developers. The Peel Liaison Committee of the Urban Development Institute, which included most of the principal players in the local development industry, submitted a brief strongly endorsing regional government, although there was no comment on Streetsville's position.[12] Those developers who did write individually were also favourably disposed to the January 23 announcement. Where concerns were raised, they were usually accompanied by requests for minor boundary modifications to ensure that a company's land holdings could remain within one municipality. The March 30, 1973, submission of H. Peter Langer, executive vice president of Markborough Properties, was typical:

> We fully support the proposals as set out in the pamphlet published by your Ministry. In particular, we are most anxious that the proposed boundary between Southern Peel and Central Peel should not be shifted south, as we wish our lands to remain within one municipality. This will permit a more orderly and speedier development of our lands than would be the case if our lands were situated in the separate municipalities.[13]

Markborough may have had a more direct interest in the Streetsville question than this correspondence reveals. A series of handwritten notes, put together by unidentified civil servants not long after Darcy McKeough's 1969 Halton-Peel proposal was released, summarized the views of the various municipalities and some other key players. It was noted that Markborough was "not counting on Stsvl for services—wish to proceed on annexation."[14]

Meanwhile, Bruce McLaughlin, the powerful developer whose Mississauga-based company owned most of the land around the centre of that municipality, was insisting in newspaper interviews that "it is ideal that Streetsville and Port Credit come together [with Mississauga] to form one new system-planned city."[15]

Darcy McKeough, who was out of cabinet for most of 1973, recalls that when he was minister of municipal affairs a number of land developers—including some of the big players in Mississauga—were frequently engaged in informal discussions with him and his cabinet colleagues. Sometimes, ministry bureaucrats would be invited to these meetings so that a back-and-forth discussion could take place, allowing the minister to better assess the various suggestions. McKeough does not remember whether there were specific discussions about Streetsville or regional government. He also notes that there was never anything that was not above board about these discussions. "I got tremendous advice, practical advice, and not self-serving advice" from the participants, the former minister states. "There were some good people."[16]

The proposal ratified by cabinet did make reference to a positive spin-off for the business sector by claiming that "the improvements in the municipal structure should provide a clearer, more consistent planning and development policy, and thereby assist the process of development by the private sector in the area."[17]

The provincial government's public statements were sometimes ambiguous about how restructuring would affect the developers. When he released the proposals, Arthur Meen assured residents that, "By merging adjacent municipalities and broadening the responsibilities of local administrations, we also hope to discourage the traditional old scramble for assessment."[18] The night after the announcement, Davis defended the proposals at a meeting of his riding association. The *Toronto Star* reported that the premier assured his audience that the changes would help control urban sprawl:* "I will not see concrete highways and asphalt stretching all the way

---

* John White made similar arguments in his correspondence to residents in the affected areas: "Regional government will assist in the effort to protect green space for ourselves and future generations. It will be possible to share assessment over wide areas making it possible to preserve rural and open areas by enabling the agricultural community to share in the more lucrative tax base of the urban and industrial areas" (Archives of Ontario, RG 3-49, tb 38, Davis General Correspondence, 1973).

from Yonge Street in Toronto to Main Street in Brampton."[19] The *Globe and Mail* noted, however, that Davis reminded the attendees about the South Peel Water and Sewage System, and stated that the area's rapid growth would not have been possible without such a regionally oriented project.[20]

STREETSVILLE MOBILIZES

Streetsville, meanwhile, was determined to assertively oppose the province's proposal. "This is a can of worms," declared McCallion as she left Mohawk College. She refused, however, to be pinned down on what action her municipality might take.[21]

That became more apparent at the January 29 meeting of town council. About 70 people packed the small chamber to hear their elected officials take turns denouncing the provincial announcement—which, considering the public's support for the SCORE petition in the spring of 1972, was almost certainly a view shared by most residents.

The town's strategy boiled down to the following: to hold a "referendum" (actually a plebiscite, because the results could not be legally binding) on the town's future; to support a citizens' coalition similar to SCORE; and to appeal directly to the member of provincial parliament for Peel North, William Grenville Davis.

Was this all a shell game? Did Streetsville's local leaders know that the inevitable result would be the town's loss of municipal status? Did they wage the fight as a mere concession to public opinion? Jack Graham argues in the affirmative. He believes that Streetsville council was "intellectually dishonest" in pursuing the cause, and that the municipal politicians had a duty to communicate to their constituents that "this is it; this is reality. My feeling is you face it and you get the best deal you can from it."

The former mayor is convinced that opposing amalgamation was simply an expedient calculation. "Politically, you couldn't lose on that one," Graham remarks. "Everybody in town would vote for you because you are going to save the town!"[22]

If Streetsville council believed that the town was unlikely to survive, hoisting the white flag would arguably not have been the only honest option. If prosecuted with sincerity and principle, a spirited campaign to express deep reservations, to question the government's motives, and to attempt to show that there are viable alternatives, can be considered a legitimate course of action. For her part, Gianna Williams, editor of the *Review*, conceded that she was "very pessimistic" about Streetsville's chances. She nevertheless strongly exhorted her readers to continue the battle. "We are manipulated every day of our lives into a lifestyle selected by a few people," she observed. "Isn't it about time we stopped [merely] talking about it?"[23]

There may have even been some justification for optimism. Ron Walker, chairman of the Streetsville Public Utilities Commission, noted that strong, concerted citizen action could compel the government to change its mind. He recalled the successful effort by many Toronto residents to stop the construction of the Spadina Expressway.[24] Needless to say, the expressway's opponents had been accused in many quarters (prior to their victory) of wasting time on a lost cause.

Walker could have added that Halton county council's 1972 submission to the province had also recommended only three lower-tier municipalities, but Milton persisted, and, in the January 23 announcement, the province had agreed that Milton should be an expanded fourth Halton municipality, taking in part of what then belonged to the Town of Oakville and all of the Township of Nassagaweya. Arthur Meen's remarks about Milton could almost as easily have been made about Streetsville:

> Having considered both sides of the question very carefully, we are inclined to see considerable merit in Milton's point of view. We agree that there is a separate, identifiable community of interest centred

upon Milton.... We see it as having a character and prospects for development similar to those of the proposed Area Municipality of Central Peel.[25]

All told, many residents genuinely believed that they could get through to Davis. If he had been able (as was the common perception) to put the brakes on McKeough's Halton-Peel proposals of 1969-70, when he was still only the minister of education, why could he not come to the rescue of his constituents again as premier?

The Mississauga politicians, meanwhile, quickly dismissed Streetsville's efforts. As the latter municipality was finalizing its strategy, Lou Parsons was urging Davis to resist his constituents' lobbying. In a January 29 letter to the premier, the Mississauga reeve and former county warden wrote:

> I fully realize the very difficult position which you personally find yourself in as the Member for Peel North particularly as it applies to the citizens of Streetsville. I do not, however, share the concerns expressed by the lady Mayor of that Municipality that the majority of people in Streetsville are pitted against a Government that does not respond to local opinion. It is my belief that the Mayor has overplayed her hand and that in fact given time, fair encouragement and a congenial welcome, the citizens of Streetsville will become very happy citizens in the new municipality which will be created as a result of your Government's proposals.[26]

In the same letter, Parsons also assured Davis that he would work "to strengthen [the premier's] hand" by getting most of the Peel municipalities onside.

Streetsville's new citizens' group was named SPUR— Streetsville's Place Under Regionalism. Its executive, headed by architect Vic Dale, included several other prominent residents, among them Blake Goodings who had led the SCORE campaign. There were no politicians on the executive; Streetsville's council no doubt wished to avoid being accused by the province and the media of engineering a battle to allow the politicians to keep their posts.

Reflecting on SPUR's efforts, Dale insists that Streetsville's stand was neither rooted in reactionary sentimentalism nor characterized by a fundamental aversion to change. He argues that residents knew that major changes and land developments were coming, but "they wanted to have some control over it."[27]

Many citizens did, indeed, demonstrate an unusually high level of understanding about what was happening and what the options were—and their motives appear to have been more than parochial. The resistance in Streetsville did not spring from what the *London Free Press* described as the "Davis government's inability to get its intention across to the people, especially those in predominantly rural areas with in-bred suspicions of the big government trend."[28] University student Doug Flowers, who would later play a pivotal role in the Streetsville downtown renewal initiative, expressed some sophisticated, yet widely held, views in a 1972 letter to provincial Management Board Chairman Charles MacNaughton:

> I have come to recognize, as does the Toronto-Centred Plan, the bene-
> fit of retaining existing communities in the face of impending develop-
> ment. This town is a public, not a mass, it is aware and concerned, its
> citizens participate because they have an identity and a sense of com-
> munity.... [R]elationships develop quickly in this town and conse-
> quently there is a high degree of social stability ... I am honestly over-
> whelmed by the degree of social concern and commitment to people
> that the leaders of Streetsville exhibit. It is my personal belief that should
> Streetsville be expanded, the future residents of the new community will
> benefit not only from a high-degree of people-oriented planning but
> also from a rare community spirit which emanates from the town.[29]

Nor was this the classic urban-suburban annexation battle, in which self-interested suburban residents wanted to avoid having to subsidize the city's higher social costs. Although Mississauga's pop-ulation was much larger than Streetsville's, the latter was certainly not more wealthy;* and although Goodings and Dale contended that Streetsville's services and fiscal management were better than Mississauga's, they consistently insisted that the people of Streetsville did not want to be absorbed by Mississauga even if it could be demonstrated that they would pay lower taxes.†

THE REFERENDUM REQUEST
AND MEEN'S VISIT TO STREETSVILLE

Special permission for a plebiscite was required under the *Municipal Elections Act, 1972*. The Act permitted municipalities to hold such a vote on their own accord if it was scheduled for the same day as a municipal election. At other times, this case included, the consent of the Ontario Municipal Board had to be sought.

Clerk-administrator Len McGillivary quickly got to work with town solicitor Ward Allen (a Toronto lawyer retained on a part-time basis by Streetsville) to draft the request. Streetsville's application

---

* Streetsville's average family income in 1971 was $11,757, and the median was $11,206. The figures for Mississauga were $13,034 and $12,826, respectively. Streetsville's numbers were approximately at the levels for the Toronto metropolitan area, although the town's median was slightly higher. See Statistics Canada, *1971 Census of Canada— Census Tract Bulletin (Toronto): Population and Housing Characteristics by Census Tracts*, pp. 136-139.

† In his open letter (*op. cit.*), Ron Walker attempted to demonstrate that the Streetsville P.U.C.'s financial position was better than that of its Mississauga counterpart, but he added that, "These are only facts and figures. If they were reversed, I would still fight for Streetsville and I think that you would too." In a 1972 article summarizing SCORE's efforts, Goodings acknowledged that the owner of a home assessed at $30,000 would pay somewhat less in property taxes in Mississauga than in Streetsville. He argued, however, that, "To me quality of life is more important than an additional $26.10 in taxes each year. We have something rather intangible but very special in Streetsville. Let's keep it." ("SCORE", *Booster*, April 5, 1972.)

focussed on citizens' right to be heard on an important issue and insisted that town council desired to receive input from its constituents. The question before the voters would be, "Are you in favour of the Municipal Council of the Town of Streetsville requesting the Government of Ontario to form Streetsville and adjacent lands as an additional area municipality within the proposed Peel Region?" Voting day was to be March 28, 1973, with advance polls on March 21 and 24.

"The Ballot on March 28th will be the most important Ballot to take place since Streetsville was incorporated in 1858, 10 years prior to the incorporation [sic] of the Province of Ontario," declared the *Streetsville Review* in an article based closely on a municipal press release. "As has been the record of Streetsville in the past, the Council is leaving no stone unturned in its efforts to have informed citizen participation in the decision-making process."[30]

To facilitate this process, Streetsville opened a "Referendum Information Centre" on February 27, at 184 Queen Street South. Treasurer Emmaleen Sabourin was put in charge, and her town-hall hours were adjusted accordingly (the centre was open Monday to Friday from noon until 9 p.m. and Saturdays from 9 a.m. to 1 p.m.).

The mayor moved her office—by then more like a command post—to the centre, enabling her to converse with interested citizens. Some of the $5,000 which council had set aside to hold the referendum was to be spent on the centre, which was largely staffed by volunteers.

It would be partly, but not entirely, accurate to brand the information centre as the *de facto* headquarters for the anti-amalgamation campaign in Streetsville. McCallion did write to parliamentary assistant Arthur Meen inviting the province to send information promoting its arguments. He appears to have obliged, because copies of the January 23 announcement and summaries were available.[31]

With a showdown looming, Meen ventured into Streetsville on February 15, 1973, for a three-and-a-half-hour meeting with Streetsville council and representatives of SPUR. At his request, the meeting was closed to the public. Meen had been delegated to hold discussions in most of the affected municipalities during the several weeks after the Mohawk College announcement. He was also entrusted with telling Streetsville that the province would oppose the town's application to the OMB for permission to hold the plebiscite.

Meen's visit went badly. His discussions with the council had hardly commenced before he found himself grappling for answers when challenged to refute Streetsville's longstanding position that it should be an expanded, yet separate, municipality. He was apparently not familiar with the *Boundary Study* of 1968.

Meen did, of course, come armed with some rebuttals. An obvious query pertained to the proposal to merge Halton's seven municipalities into four, while Peel's 10 municipalities would be consolidated into just three. Any significant growth in Milton and north Oakville, he pointed out, was at least 25 years away, whereas growth around Streetsville was imminent. Streetsville's small staff could not possibly be required to assume such responsibilities, whereas Mississauga's much larger administration could easily absorb Streetsville and Port Credit.

What about the wishes of the people of Streetsville? Was public opinion in the town not almost unanimous for maintaining Streetsville's identity? Meen agreed that sentiments in Streetsville were strong, and he professed sympathy with the desire to maintain the town's identity. He cautioned, however, that no practical scenario could permit Streetsville to remain as it had been. Big changes were coming. New developments were being planned. What was needed, the parliamentary assistant reasoned, was a strong, large municipality which could deal with these pressures.[32]

"It was one of the worst meetings of my career," Ron Farrow

reminisces. The now-retired public servant remembers counselling Meen not to claim that specific services would definitely improve, but to present the case based on general equalization principles and argue that the consolidated municipalities would have an enhanced capacity to deal effectively with area-wide problems.*

Farrow recalls being delayed by inclement weather. "When I arrived, [Meen] had just finished saying, 'Well, Your Worship, there'll be all sorts of improvements to your services. Mr. Farrow is here and he can explain that.'

"I started into some bafflegab," Farrow continues, insisting that he had a high regard for Meen and understands how, in the frenzied world of politics, "briefings can sometimes go in one ear and out the other." In this case, "it was just as if I had a hole dug for me. It was not one of those meetings when you walk out and say, 'That went rather well!'"[33]

As the Friday, March 9, date for the OMB hearing neared, visible resistance to the proposals was increasing. "Now is the time to take off the gloves and fight," screamed a front-page article in the *Review*.[34] In

---

* A later (undated) briefing note prepared by the Local Government Organization Branch, probably for the premier's June visit to Streetsville, dealt with several anticipated questions and objections. The first was, "How will Streetsville services improve under regional government?" The paper stated, "This question was asked before and there was considerable confusion and misunderstanding on this issue." Here is how the civil servants wanted that question answered: "Local government reform will provide a basis for more comprehensive decision-making since elected councils will be responsible for governing a wider area. However, since the decisions about the quality of services are made by the elected councillors, it will be their decision as to what changes are to be made in local services. The new Peel legislation provides a framework for local government but it does not make decisions about service quality. Consequently, the Provincial Government cannot make predictions about future quality of services" (Archives of Ontario, RG 19-131, tb 7).

an open letter to the residents of Streetsville, SPUR's Residents' Action Committee made some arguments that would be constantly repeated during discussions on regional government:

> [O]ur influence, our say as to what we want as a way of life will be lost. As the matter now stands, and which would continue under an expanded Streetsville Area Municipality, we have the ear of our representatives and we can usually get things done in our best interest because Council knows we won't for long tolerate it otherwise. Under a government with jurisdiction over all of South Peel, our representation, and thus control over our own destiny, will be assimilated and decided by politicians who cannot identify with our collective philosophies.[35]

A number of members of Streetsville's large Portuguese minority were among those who expressed their desire not to lose Streetsville. Joe Simoes argued that the town was "precious" to its residents and that, "We accept the plan of regionalism but [wish to] have Streetsville as a fourth municipality instead of the three areas now planned."[36]

A "Calling All Streetsville Young People" petition was even initiated by some local scouts. It stated, "We the children of the town of Streetsville ... do not wish to become part of Mississauga but wish to maintain a separate community and keep the advantages that Streetsville has to offer."[37]

The Streetsville Historical Society likewise joined the action. President Vince Hyland, who had moved to Streetsville from Cooksville five years earlier, appealed to Davis: "As a native son of a nearby community, Brampton, you are doubtless well aware that Streetsville was pioneered in 1818 and throughout its long history has figured prominently in the commercial, cultural, industrial and political leadership of Peel County."[38]

Hyland's colleague on the historical society, Mary Manning, who had established herself as a respected writer and local historian, also voiced her opposition to the scheme, adding that her ancestors were solid Conservatives at a time when the Liberals were guaranteed to win in the area even if they had fielded a dog as a candidate. "Let's hope that the Conservatives have not become the 'dog,'" Manning wrote, in what was, for her, a rare departure from the standards of utmost politeness.[39]

Streetsville's case suffered a setback at county council on February 19, when the majority voted against deferring discussion of Peel's official response to the provincial proposal. Disagreement erupted over whether Streetsville had previously assured the county that it would have its brief ready for the meeting. "We indicated that we would try to have it in," McCallion protested. Mississauga's Lou Parsons took issue with the Streetsville mayor. The deferral motion was defeated and the government's position was affirmed[40]—it was, after all, virtually identical to what Parsons had steered through the county council the previous summer. The brief which the county eventually sent to Toronto proposed only very minor modifications to what the province had put forward.[41]

THE O.M.B. HEARING AND THE PETITION TO CABINET

Norma Lynes was one of several dozen Streetsville residents present in the Ontario Municipal Board Hearing Room on Friday, March 9, at 123 Edward St. in Toronto. She recalls that the spokespeople for Streetsville presented themselves confidently, eloquently, and with conviction. Lynes was rooting strongly for the town. As a former trustee with the Town of Weston Board of Education, she had witnessed that municipality's absorption by the Borough of York. Having moved to Streetsville a short time later, she recalls that she sensed that "now we would see the same thing happening all over again."[42] In a letter she wrote that month to Davis, Lynes opined that "it would have been easy for our Mayor to have dealt us in (and probably to her personal advantage), but she and her council have committed themselves to the wishes of the people they represent. Citizenry and local government unite to ask you to take a long second look at the situation."[43]

Streetsville's witnesses at the five-hour hearing were Mayor McCallion, Clerk McGillivary, Gianna Williams (from both the *Streetsville Review* and the historical society), and SPUR representatives Vic Dale, Blake Goodings, Bob Keeping, and Paul Chase. Mississauga Clerk John Corney appeared on behalf of his municipality. Streetsville resident Emerson Tapley came to argue against the application, insisting that the cost could not be justified.

Streetsville had to face some tough opposition. Mississauga solicitor Len Stewart vigorously contested the application. Streetsville's Ward Allen called on the OMB not to allow Mississauga to have standing at the hearing, saying that this was a matter of relevance only to the people of Streetsville. The OMB disagreed.

Stewart's brief to the board was very sharply worded. "[T]his plebiscite is an unnecessary, pointless, pernicious practice," he asserted. "How can an elector intelligently assess the question without knowing *what lands, whose lands*, and more importantly how much adjacent land, 1 acre, 10 acres, 1,000 acres or 10,000 acres, its general boundaries, and in what adjacent municipalities[?]" Stewart argued that the plebiscite would be on an issue which was not within municipal jurisdiction. But if the "Council [of Streetsville] has power to act, the Council is attempting to substitute the direct decision of the electors for that of the Council to which the law has assigned it [and therefore] the vote [would be] illegal."[44]

Streetsville contended that the question was *intra vires* the municipality because council was seeking formal public feedback on the position *the town* should take in its representations to the provincial government. Moreover, if Mississauga was correct in its insistence that a plebiscite amounted to an abrogation of council's duties, then such a vote would be unjustifiable at any time and on any issue, in which case provincial law would not even entertain the possibility.

The province was an important intervener. John Bell of the Ministry of the Treasury, Economics and Intergovernmental Affairs argued that a referendum would serve no purpose, would oversimplify the complex issues involved, and that Streetsville was free to submit a brief to the province without such a vote.*

The two OMB members who heard the application were R.M. McGuire, one of the board's several vice chairmen, and Allan Van Every, a former Toronto Township councillor who had a Port Credit law practice. They quickly dismissed Streetsville's request, offering the following explanation:

> There has [sic] been presented basically three submissions as to why a referendum should be permitted as requested, and they are:
>
> (1) That the results of the referendum would provide a more appropriate manner to inform the Provincial Government of the attitude of the people of the municipality.
>
> (2) That it will provide direction to the municipal council as to what submission it should make respecting its position in the proposed new Regional Government.
>
> (3) That it will provide the encouragement for the electors to inform themselves on the issue.
>
> Dealing with these in order, firstly the provincial statements and policy enunciations indicate encouragement for participation but

---

* At a Progressive Conservative "mid-term conference" on September 19, 1973, Premier Davis offered a similar argument, insisting that "if you open up one community to a referendum, you have to do likewise in other communities." He added that, "Government can never abdicate its responsibility to govern" (Archives of Ontario, Clare Westcott recordings, F 2094-8-0-58).

not by means of a referendum as proposed. The Board is governed by provincial policy when enunciated by the responsible Minister.

In respect to the second submission, the evidence clearly indicates that the municipal council is not in any doubt as to its mandate and will in fact be making some submission even before the results are known.

Dealing with the last one, it is unnecessary to use this tool to inform the public, but the informing of the public is a very worthwhile exercise....[45]

"We're darn mad, Bill Davis," wrote Blake Goodings and Vic Dale following the hearing.[46] Streetsville briefly considered setting up a special trust company to get around the *Municipal Elections Act* and hold a referendum anyway. McCallion, looking back, says that this option was rejected because it would have lacked legitimacy.[47] Streetsville did, however, petition cabinet to overturn the OMB's ruling. This request was quickly rejected on March 21, 1973.

Bob Keeping, who was assisting SPUR, recalls that seeking permission for a plebiscite was a win-win strategy. Any vote would likely show that an overwhelming majority of residents were in favour of the town's position. A denial of the request to conduct the vote would be confirmation of the province's arrogance and would indirectly reinforce the validity of Streetsville's position.[48]

STREETSVILLE'S REPORT TO THE PROVINCE

Streetsville's brief[49] was finally submitted on March 30, one day before the deadline. Council delivered it in person to Arthur Meen and reviewed it with him, page by page, in a two-and-a-half-hour meeting.[50] In a letter written a few days later, McCallion advised Minister John White that, "I have asked to hear from Art after his staff have had time to review the Brief, and he assured me that this would be done within the next two weeks." She added that, "It is obvious that once the major responsibilities have been transferred to the Regional Council, the Area Councils should be structured so that they can more easily and effectively relate to the people of the community." McCallion also made brief reference to a discussion which she had with White at an event the week prior, and she assured the minister that the maps and other data in Streetsville's submission "will give you the information you requested."[51]

The Streetsville report included some arguments which the town had put forward on earlier occasions: that the community was well managed, could run a larger area, and that the proposed South Peel municipality was too large for any meaningful exercise in local government. The proposed boundaries of Streetsville departed somewhat from the 1968 *Boundary Study*. Gone, for example, were that report's recommendations that Streetsville's town centre would eventually move to a new location southwest of the existing town site and that Streetsville's eastern boundary would be the Credit River. Instead, the current Town of Streetsville would, presumably, be the town centre for the expanded area, which would extend east almost to the First Line (McLaughlin Road). As for its southern boundary, Streetsville offered two options—either the proposed Highway 403 or Dundas Street (west of the Credit River only). Streetsville explained that this change conformed to more-recent developments, such as the boundaries of the proposed Erin Mills community.

One of the arguments put forward by Streetsville's opponents in Mississauga and at Queen's Park was that the administrators of a small community could not possibly be adequately equipped to serve a much larger municipality. In attempting to refute this objection, Streetsville's brief went into great detail extolling the credentials and experience of the town's managers—including, among others, Clerk Len McGillivary, Treasurer Emmaleen Sabourin, Director of Works Keith Cowan, and Police Chief Don Fletcher. A

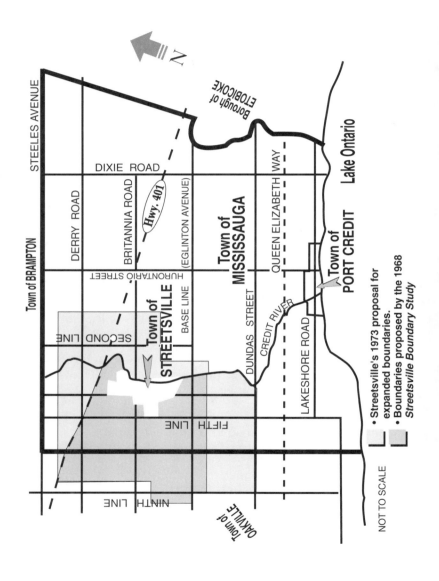

detailed description of Streetsville's services was also provided—the fact that it had far more daycare spaces per capita than Mississauga, that it had a good arena and community centre, competitive utility rates, and a library which could serve 25,000 people. The report favoured centralized regional administration for certain police functions, but advocated the continuation of local police forces.

Appended to the Streetsville submission was a report by MacGillivray and Company (chartered accountants, no relation to the town clerk) praising the management practices of the town, its financial health, and its approach to planning. These consultants insisted that "both existing residents and newcomers are going to be significantly better off, financially, living in a community where the existing debt structure is low, growth is controlled, and development is made to pay its own way."* An accompanying chart presented a comparison of per capita expenditures in Streetsville and Mississauga, showing Streetsville as being at least as efficient as Mississauga in most categories. However, two sets of numbers were underlined by the officials at Queen's Park who reviewed the report. The "General Administration" category showed Streetsville spending $19.62 per capita, compared with $8.67 in Mississauga. In "Parks and Recreation," Streetsville was spending $3.68 for

---

* Streetsville prided itself on its development levies, which amounted to $1,100 per house and $475 per apartment unit. Critics allege that such policies lead to higher prices and indirectly discourage the construction of housing for modest-income families. The consultants attempted to refute the first of these criticisms. "It has been argued that such a `hard-line' policy inflates the cost of housing. It could be equally logically argued that such a policy really only reduces the speculative profit in the land, in that the price of housing is set in a much wider area by the free market. Although the discussion is academic, the [positive] consequences for the ratepayer are most significant." This statement does not, of course, directly address the second criticism. There were almost no homes in Streetsville which could be termed "monster homes" or estates,

every resident, compared with $17.33 in Mississauga. Provincial staff may have seen this last disparity as an indication that Streetsville's services in that category were not adequate. However, part of the difference can probably be accounted for by the arena's status as a separate, non-profit corporation.

Perhaps one of Streetsville's most important arguments—almost ignored by the submission except for two brief references (page 6, "closer representation by population" and "no domination of the region by one municipality, group or interest")—was that a fourth lower-tier municipality would help to correct the lack of representation by population in the proposed region. Otherwise, a South Peel municipality (Mississauga-Streetsville-Port Credit) would have two thirds of the population but only 46 percent of the seats on regional council. Setting up a fourth municipality (Greater Streetsville) could ensure that no municipality would have control of regional council, while permitting, in the not-too-distant future (as development continued), a representation formula in keeping with each municipality's population. Surprisingly, in a point-by-point review of the province's proposal, Streetsville *endorsed* the

---

and there were many modest dwellings and rental units. However, most of the dwellings had been built before the development levies were instituted. Mississauga did not have blanket development levies, although it was proceeding with plans in 1973 to extract $50 per unit from the developers ("Levy on developers will provide amenities," *Mississauga Times*, January 31, 1973). Mississauga already had special agreements with the major developers for sewers and sidewalks to be constructed, but not for services external to the developments such as community centres. By late 1972, Mississauga councillors were claiming that they faced a financial squeeze, and they were urging the province to provide assistance. Lou Parsons warned that there would be a "severe curtailment of growth" if such aid was not forthcoming. ("Warn of curbs on Mississauga development if province can't increase aid," *Globe and Mail*, December 14, 1972.)

province's representation formula for the regional council. The report offered no recommendation for how many seats the new Streetsville should get.

It is possible that Streetsville sidestepped the representation issue because some of Minister White's correspondence to local residents had pointed out that an expanded Streetsville would not immediately solve the rep.-by-pop. problem; Mississauga would still have a majority of residents, without a majority of seats.[52] However, if the Streetsville scheme had been accepted, and assuming that population growth patterns had remained the same, Mississauga would today have about 400,000 people, Streetsville 225,000, Brampton 320,000, and Caledon 48,000.

Predictably, the Town of Mississauga was not impressed with Streetsville's submission. It delivered a fiery rebuttal, disputing virtually every argument made by Streetsville and decrying what it perceived as Streetsville's offensive tactics. "This is all a lot of nonsense" was a recurring sentence in the Mississauga document. Mississauga also claimed that amalgamation would reduce taxes in Streetsville (a prediction which did not materialize, as Streetsville residents were required to pay considerably more in 1974).

As for Streetsville's position that "with only minor staff additions, the present administrative structure of Streetsville will be able to more-than-adequately perform the necessary functions," Mississauga was very critical: "If a Town of 7,000 people has a staff who with only 'minor staff additions' would be capable of serving a population as proposed in the expanded municipality, isn't there something wrong? It is inconceivable that a municipality of 7,000 would have such a staff." Also ridiculed was Streetsville's promise that, "It will be a continuing policy of the Area Municipality of South Peel West [Streetsville] to take advantage of the wide range of skills which are available from consultants rather than burden the taxpayers with expensive overhead costs as a result of experts on staff being used for part of any year of operation." Mississauga argued that amalgamation would allow Streetsville residents to benefit from the services of permanent, experienced professionals, rather than having "a seasonally run municipality."[53]

Sarcasm and exaggeration aside, this last point was not without merit, and the provincial bureaucrats actually underlined it in one of their copies. Indeed, Streetsville itself had made efforts to lessen its reliance on *ad-hoc* consulting, in favour of more-permanent, ongoing professional advice and administration. In 1971, for example, council passed a resolution to advertise for the newly created position of director of works and planning, with a salary of $17,000 per annum. The public statement accompanying the resolution presented several justifications for such a recruitment, including the need "to have staff available to make recommendations to Council, making the Town less dependent upon outside Consultants, such as Planning and Engineering, thus reducing their current consulting fees to the Town."[54]

FORMER MAYOR GRAHAM'S VIEWS

Jack Graham, the former Streetsville mayor who had been receptive to a merger with Mississauga, kept a low public profile on the issue in 1973. Behind the scenes, however, he was taking a keen interest. On March 20, 1973, he wrote to Arthur Meen, assuring the government that it need not worry about what was happening in Streetsville: "Every effort has been made to generate public support within the community for the position taken by the Mayor and Council and frankly, the reaction has been minimal." Graham also advised the government that he "detect[ed] a public reaction against the local political people," because they chose to persist in petitioning cabinet to overturn the OMB ruling and because they had thus far decided not to participate in discussions with Port Credit and Mississauga to work out the details of the amalgamation.

Enclosed with the March 20 letter was another letter, eight pages long, dated January 30, 1973. Graham explained that he delayed sending the earlier correspondence because "there appeared to be some considerable activity taking place in Streetsville." He added, however, that after further assessing the situation he was convinced his original analysis was valid.

In the January letter, Graham noted that before he "voluntarily retired" as mayor in 1969, he had supported amalgamation and continued to do so. He assured Meen, however, that the letter's observations were sincere and objective. "Although it is difficult to judge and difficult to really know, I frankly very sincerely suspect that the large majority of the people in Streetsville are willing to accept the present proposal of the Province of Ontario, perhaps in some cases quite reluctantly, but nevertheless to accept it and to have the matter completed as proposed." The former mayor added that, "I have come to this conclusion by my observation of the modus operandi of the present Mayor of Streetsville and her supporters."

Graham dismissed the efforts of SCORE and SPUR. He noted that during the 1972 SCORE campaign he had devoted a Sunday to driving down every street in the town with another former local politician in order to count the number of houses displaying SCORE signs. There were, wrote Graham, only 149.

Graham gave no heed to the 1972 SCORE petition, which was signed by an overwhelming majority of Streetsville's adult residents: "The petition was circulated and signed, and as is the usual case, I understand a fair number of people signed it who do not live in the Town of Streetsville. I would make no further comment in regards to petitions, as quite frankly, I have learned to place very little, if any value in a document of this nature." A few pages later, Graham emphatically asserted that, "It is difficult to assess the feelings of the balance of the community [by which he meant those who have not actively participated in lobbying the provincial government] whom, as you can appreciate, represent the vast majority of the people. We have not taken a poll or a plebiscite or had any overt expression of their opinion...."

Graham advised Meen that criticism of the provincial proposal was coming from three groups in the community: those who were "politically involved"; the "sports oriented people," who above all feared losing the community centre, which had been built using the donations of many Streetsville residents; and the "old residents" who had been born and raised in the community. Graham expressed sympathy with the last group, albeit somewhat off-hand-edly; he reminded Meen that it is common for people in their "twilight years" to be reticent in the face of change.

Graham capped off his letter thus: "May I say in conclusion that Streetsville is 'Bill Davis territory' and that I am more than willing to place a personal wager with you that when this thing is all over and the next election rolls along, the decision you make in regards to this matter either one way or the other won't cost Bill Davis more than five votes. I give you two to one on this and you can name the amount."

Meen sent a copy of the two letters to Davis, although he blanked out the first two paragraphs of the January letter (I have not found an original). "I think you will find it interesting and helpful," the parliamentary secretary assured the premier. Meen requested a meeting with Davis to discuss Graham's position, but the premier declined.[55]

How much influence Graham's correspondence had is difficult to gauge. Were the parliamentary assistant and the premier aware of the internal dynamics of Streetsville politics, including the bitter relationship between Graham and McCallion? Did Davis decline to meet with Meen because he had already made up his mind, because he was pressed for time, or was it because he believed that he already had a good sense of Streetsville opinion?

Whether or not Graham's representations were of any consequence, there are some puzzling comments in the former mayor's correspondence which merit examination. His assertion that he delayed sending the January letter because there appeared to be "some considerable activity taking place" (which, according to Graham, later fizzled out) might seem insignificant until it is recalled that Streetsville, at that time, decided to seek permission to hold a plebiscite. Although this could be merely a coincidence, Graham only sent the letter once the plebiscite request was rejected by the OMB, and therefore after it became unlikely that his own assessment of public opinion could be disproved by an official vote of the residents.

Graham's dismissal of the SCORE petition is problematic. It is true that some residents might not have appreciated what they were signing. It is likewise the case that a petition is not a secret ballot, meaning that signatories might not always be offering an honest expression of their views. Nevertheless, when a petition manages to garner thousands of signatures, should it not, in a healthy democracy, be given at least some consideration rather than summarily dismissed? As for Graham's assertion that some signatories were not Streetsville residents, the SCORE co-ordinators readily admitted this—indeed, they emphasized it. After all, Streetsville's position was that it and *adjacent lands* should form a separate lower-tier municipality. The SCORE people claimed that a few hundred residents of the northwest quadrant of the Town of Mississauga had also signed on, indicating their willingness to be part of Streetsville, a community to which they gravitated for many services and activities.[56]

The former mayor's characterization of the supporters of town council's position also begs comment. Even if the "politically involved" people, the "old residents," and the "sports oriented" people were the only ones who opposed the province's plan, this would not have been an inconsequential cohort. The number of people in Streetsville who were engaged in some sort of local political activity was not to be written off. Many citizens served on committees, boards, and commissions. Executive members of the chamber of commerce were also keenly interested in municipal politics, as were many service club members and the executive members of the Portuguese Canadian Integration Movement. The number of sports-oriented people was also significant. Graham himself noted that he was a financial contributor to the arena, as had been a high proportion of Streetsville residents. Many families, moreover, had children enrolled in minor-league sports in town. A March 1973 anti-amalgamation petition, which was circulated among parents whose children belonged to the Streetsville Minor Hockey Association, garnered 316 signatures.[57]

The "old residents" were certainly a diminishing minority, but many Streetsville people have emphatically insisted to me that those who had moved to the community as adults were at least as opposed as the old-timers to having Streetsville absorbed by Mississauga. Streetsville was a special place in which they found a unique community spirit and civic pride. Among those who held (and continue to hold) this view is Elizabeth Colley, who in a letter dated March 22, 1972, advised Davis as follows:

I come originally from Alberta, but have lived in five provinces of Canada and in Great Britain. And never have I experienced a sense of true neighbourhoodness and community spirit such as I have found here in Streetsville.

Although writing as a private citizen and one who voted you into office, I find my position [as librarian] in Streetsville gives me a unique opportunity to talk with all manner of citizens. I can assure you that my dismay at the threatened take-over is shared not only by those born here and living here all their lives but perhaps even more by those of us who have deliberately chosen to settle here because we value the quality of life in Streetsville.[58]

Graham's charge that the Streetsville politicians were irresponsible for not participating in meetings to iron out the logistics of amalgamation with Mississauga and Port Credit would only have been valid had Streetsville endorsed amalgamation. To have engaged in such discussions so early would have completely undermined Streetsville's official position.* At that point, the province had not even introduced any legislation.

Looking back on the events of the late 1960s and early 1970s, Graham is still convinced that amalgamation was necessary and inevitable. But he now emphatically says that public opinion against it was very strong in Streetsville: "There was a very, very emotional atmosphere. I don't think there was a citizen in the community who didn't want to preserve the community.

"If I had decided to stay [in active local politics] I wouldn't be elected as dogcatcher," the former mayor exclaims. "There wouldn't be two votes. I don't think even my wife would vote for me!"[59]

OTHER VIEWS ON STREETSVILLE

The most outspoken academic commentator on the proposed Peel regional government was Desmond Morton, a well-known, left-leaning history professor, who was then at the University of Toronto's Erindale College. Morton, who later that year released a book on Mayor William Holmes Howland and the Toronto reform

---

* On Friday, March 16, 1973, there was a "Regional Government Meeting" involving six Mississauga staff members, three provincial civil servants, and Port Credit town manager Bill Munden. The Town of Mississauga council subsequently adopted the report from this meeting and made it the municipality's official submission to the provincial government, with the additional recommendation "that the province be requested to provide that the responsibility for Library Boards be transferred to the area councils," as opposed to remaining under a special-purpose body. (Archives of Ontario, RG 19-131, tb 6.)

movement of the 1880s,[60] was critical of the Davis government and the Mississauga politicians, but sympathetic to Streetsville. He wrote in one of his articles:

> The region is almost deliberately available for Metro Toronto's slop-over; it forfeits the possibility of a strong buffer between Hamilton and Toronto, and it eliminates small, genuine communities like Streetsville for the sake of three large area municipalities, none of which is really small enough to be close to the people or large enough to withstand developer pressure. To have a two-tier system for the sake of these artificial sub-units serves no visible purpose at all. Or almost no purpose, since the ambitions of a respected coterie of local and county politicians can be filled into the new regime with impressive ease.[61]

In another article, Morton observed that Streetsville was "neither rich nor exclusive," but was fighting the province because "it has the kind of sense of community which Tory politicians often talk about in speeches." He observed that "Hazel McCallion, once a pillar of local Progressive Conservatism, is now anathema to the provincial politicians and their local allies."[62]

Looking back, Morton does not regret his tough stand. He says he believed that if there had to be a regional government for Peel, additional lower-tier municipalities should have been included in the plan, because smaller municipalities often make politics more accessible, less anonymous, and encourage people to assume some responsibility for local affairs. "Democracy works better when more people participate," he remarks. As for those small municipalities that are poorly run, Morton says: "I believe it's up to public opinion to ensure that the priorities are the right ones. People are open to reason and to argument. If not, then let's give up on the democratic project."[63]

Streetsville also received a boost from two highly publicized, Peel-wide citizens' submissions. Sheridan College's Community Services Division held a forum in March 1973 called "Peel '74", bringing together influential citizens and neighbourhood activists from all parts of the county. After a day of discussion on key issues related to regional government, the participants voted 82-7 in favour of establishing a fourth municipality within Peel. (The delegates also asserted that "land speculation is a great social evil.")[64]

The Peel Association for Good Government was a widely recognized group, not affiliated with any political party, which provided thoughtful feedback on many local issues. (It is not clear, however, how many members belonged to the group or the extent of its grassroots support.) In the PAGG submission, members endorsed the regional government concept but expressed serious concerns about the representational imbalance. They recommended that this be corrected by creating a fourth municipality centred on Streetsville.[65]

Even Peel county council's support for the Queen's Park proposal proved to be far from solid. Following comments from Minister White in May that the province would not be pressing forward with the creation of regional governments in other parts of Ontario after the current round of reforms had been completed, county council approved the following resolution:

Resolved that this Council petition the Honourable John White to meet immediately with the Municipal Reorganization Committee, or County Council Committee of the Whole, to explain why the Regional Government program has been abandoned in other parts of Southern Ontario;

And further, that he be requested not to introduce the Bill on Regional Government for Peel in the House until this meeting has been held and the results transmitted to County Council.[66]

A meeting was held on May 22. Peel Warden Ivor McMullin emerged to say that White assured the county that consolidation of Ontario municipalities and the creation of regional governments would continue.[67] Nevertheless, the fact that a majority of county politicians demanded an explanation—only a few diehard regionalists like Lou Parsons and Chic Murray voted against the resolution—is an indication that support for the plan was only forthcoming out of fear that something even less desirable could be imposed.

April and May were months of decision for the government. The day after the March 31 deadline for submissions, Davis was not sounding optimistic about Streetsville's chances. In a television interview, he dismissed the mounting criticism of his regional government program in Peel and elsewhere:

> [I]t's unfortunate because in a number of areas the proposals that we presented … are not dissimilar to some of those we've had from the municipality. I mean, I am having some difficulty, I don't minimize it, with the Town of Streetsville. By and large [however] there's a degree of acceptance in the County of Peel. Our proposal for Peel County really is very similar to the proposal that the Peel County Council made to the provincial government. One could hardly describe that as imposition, lack of consultation, etc.[68]

The mayor of Streetsville believed that she had been promised by Arthur Meen that he would confer again with representatives of the town after provincial staff had an opportunity to review Streetsville's brief. Although such a subsequent discussion never did transpire, provincial staff drew up a document listing points for and against (mostly the latter) setting up a fourth municipality. The document provided some two dozen reasons for why there should not be a Greater Streetsville, most of them emphasizing that the town would not have the administrative capacity to absorb the wider area and to deal with the rapid growth expected there during the ensuing several years.[69]

However, when the same branch prepared a comprehensive internal position paper in early April, it argued that there might be advantages to creating an "optional fourth area municipality" for the new Peel Region. The officials noted that the three-municipality model

> will probably lead to strong pressures for changes in representation which would lead to one municipality having complete domination of the regional council. Such a situation would then require the creation of a fourth municipality or the establishment of a single-tier region and the elimination of the three area municipalities. If a two-tier region is preferred over the long-run then a fourth municipality should be created and not carved out later when administrative structures are well entrenched.

According to this alternative, South Peel would be divided into two municipalities, just as Streetsville was urging, but the boundaries would not be the same as those recommended in Streetsville's brief. Instead, all the lands north of Eglinton Avenue and south of the proposed boundary between South Peel and Central Peel would be part of this additional municipality. There was no explanation for the divergence from Streetsville's position, although this option in the civil servants' report was consistent with two of the alternatives prepared by the same unit in July 1972 (and discussed in the previous chapter).[70]

The formal ministerial submission to cabinet on April 13, 1973, did not entertain the option of a fourth lower-tier municipality, although much of the document was based directly on the above-mentioned position paper. The report to cabinet claimed to review "some of the more controversial parts of the proposals even in cases where no change from the original government position is recommended,"[71] but there was no discussion of Streetsville, despite the fact that Streetsville was making by far the most noise. This might be an indication that, before the matter came before the ministers, Davis had been firm—Streetsville's position would have to be resisted.

Ron Farrow speculates that Davis may have wanted to show an example in his own riding. Whereas Halton cabinet ministers Jim Snow and George Kerr had, apparently, been influential in preventing the disappearance of Milton as a municipality and in keeping Burlington with Halton, things would be different on Davis's home turf. Having the premier as its member of provincial parliament might actually have been a hindrance to Streetsville.[72]

"John White was very much in favour" of Streetsville's position, but "John White wasn't as strong as McKeough was," Hazel McCallion recalls. And both men, she believes, often had to defer to the premier. "Bill Davis controlled that cabinet. He had a smooth approach."[73]

Farrow, the bureaucrat most closely associated with the Peel file, insists he never had any indication that White was not fully on board with the January 23 proposals.[74] However, White's correspondence files contain a "personal and confidential" letter from McCallion, dated June 21, 1973 (the same day the legislation received third reading in the assembly), in which the mayor told the minister that "I want you to know how much I appreciate the effort you made on our behalf to meet the wishes of the people of Streetsville."[75]

If White was sympathetic to Streetsville's position, it would not have been out of character. The minister and Streetsville council appeared to share a skeptical attitude toward the land-development industry. To cite one example, in a February 1974 speech to the annual conference of the Ontario Association of Rural Municipalities, White had some sharp words for many development practices. At one point, he addressed himself to "developers who build shopping centres just outside the boundaries of urban municipalities," and exclaimed: "These people care not a whit for the community they purport to serve. To them a town is not a town—it's a potential market, a cluster of bodies which can be lured to any store out of town, once they're convinced that the price is right."[76] In reviewing an invitation to a luncheon seminar in August 1973, which included big names like Mississauga builder Bruce McLaughlin, White wrote a note to his executive assistant complaining that "there is a near monopoly of the developer point of view."[77] Nor was this just rhetoric. White appeared genuinely determined to bring in progressive policies, such as the much-discussed parkway belt plan and the establishment of the Niagara Escarpment Commission. The developers were not

The Honourable John H. White was Ontario's treasurer and minister of intergovernmental affairs in 1973. A widely respected and progressive politician, White is believed to have been supportive of Streetsville's position. *Photograph courtesy of Beatrice White.*

always impressed. For example, in a November 1974 letter to Davis, influential Mississauga builder Harold Shipp expressed concerns about White's approach to the land-development industry.[78]

If White did, in fact, support Streetsville's position, several factors would have curbed his chances of altering the outcome. When he was appointed treasurer and minister of economics and intergovernmental affairs, much of the groundwork had already been established; only days remained before the Mohawk College announcement. Although these proposals could have been altered in the months following their release, White did not have a great deal of time to spend on the Peel file. His portfolio was enormous, and he had to leave most of the government's consultations on regional government policies to his parliamentary assistants. In addition, White's correspondence and papers do not seem to convey that he was a powerful insider, although he did have an important position and he was a competent, principled, hard-working minister. Furthermore, White's influence may have been on the wane because it was already known he would be retiring from politics before the next election. Finally, and probably most importantly, if ever there was a time to defer to the premier, this was it. White was the MPP for London South, and he had far fewer connections in Peel than the MPP for Peel North, Bill Davis. Hazel McCallion appears to have been the only Peel politician with whom White corresponded on a first-name basis.

THE PREMIER'S STREETSVILLE VISIT AND THE DEBATE IN THE ASSEMBLY

White's personal views notwithstanding, Arthur Meen made the much-anticipated announcement on May 28. "After very careful consideration, the views put forward by the Town of Streetsville to establish a separate municipality could not be accepted," the parliamentary assistant told the legislative assembly. "It is the government of Ontario's view that the best interests of the people of Streetsville, and indeed of Port Credit also, will be served if those areas are combined with Mississauga. This will form a municipality that can bring a cohesive political and skilled full-time administrative presence to bear upon the complex problems of urban growth. Hence our decision to proceed with three area municipalities [for Peel]." Legislation would be introduced in June.[79] It appeared now that Streetsville's fate was sealed.

But town council would not take lying down what seemed like the final nail in the coffin of the Municipality of Streetsville. It passed a lengthy motion decrying the announcement, criticizing Meen for being so ill-informed during his February meeting in Streetsville, and, most important, blasting its member of provincial parliament (the premier) for not meeting with the people of Streetsville to justify the province's intentions. The motion renewed council's call for Davis to appear in the town, and it went as far as to demand his resignation as MPP for Peel North should he fail to show.

Streetsville's disgust appeared to be quite strong. The day after that resolution was passed, McCallion wrote to White, attaching the resolution and stating that, "It is unfortunate that our Member of Parliament has forced us to pass such a resolution, as we had great confidence and faith in him—a faith which has been completely shaken."[80]

Some critics of the government, such as Michael Cassidy, the NDP MPP for Ottawa Centre, described Streetsville's resolution as being "without precedent" for an Ontario municipality. This might be an overstatement, but it did reach its intended target, the Honourable Mr. Davis. The premier agreed to come to Streetsville on June 14.

When Davis and his entourage arrived at the community hall in the arena building on Church Street on that oppressively hot Thursday evening, the town was ready for him. Someone had even posted a few of Davis's old election posters below the "Welcome to Streetsville" signs. Affixed across Davis's smiling image was a big sticker with the word "SOLD!"[81] Inside the hall (which, mercifully, was air-conditioned), the premier found about 500 residents, most of them in a foul mood. When the guest of honour was introduced, a few scattered supporters rose to clap, but they were drowned out by loud "boos" and catcalls.

No doubt relieved when the crowd fell silent, Davis was soon in for another treat. The next stage guest to be welcomed was the mayor of Streetsville. The standing ovation for Hazel McCallion was loud and thunderous. Davis and the team of civil servants who accompanied him politely applauded.

The premier calmly addressed his audience. He explained that the government had to make difficult decisions and that it did not give him pleasure to see the people of Streetsville upset. He noted that much had changed in Ontario since the *Baldwin Act* of 1849. Demands for more services, the pressures of development, and the dangers of it becoming haphazard required larger units of government which could pool their resources across wider areas and benefit from larger, expert staff complements. He explained that the proposal for local government reform in Peel was favoured by the majority of Peel county council. "We did it on the basis of looking at it as objectively as we could," he assured.[82]

These explanations did not sit well with most of the audience, especially because Streetsville itself had recognized the need to expand, although without being absorbed by Mississauga. Speaker after speaker accused Davis of caving in to the big developers and the allegedly developer-friendly council of the Town of Mississauga. Others argued that Streetsville had maintained an excellent level of services and that its community spirit was second to none. Why destroy something that was working?

Davis was also asked to justify the amalgamation in light of Queen's Park's announcement on parkway belts, which took place just 10 days before the premier's visit. In his statement in the legislature, Minister White had explained that "the Southern Link [of the Parkway Belt], together with the north-south minibelts, defines and separates Oakville, Mississauga, the future Oakville north and Streetsville." He added that such a policy was needed because "a number of residential developments may fill up the land between two centres without being strongly oriented to either of them…. Experience here and elsewhere shows that satisfactory social, political and economic organization at the local level does not occur in these circumstances."[83] Streetsville residents believed this demonstrated that a separate municipal entity centred on Streetsville was justified. A few days before the Davis meeting, Reeve Robert Weylie had gone so far as to insist he was astounded that the parkway belts and the regional government announcements had come from the same man (White).[84] Davis countered that the parkway belts were not necessarily political boundaries.*

Elizabeth Hoople, a retired high school teacher, captured the sentiments of many in the crowd when she stood at the microphone and accused Davis of betraying his constituents. Norah Busby, a trustee who represented Streetsville on the Peel County Board of Education, recalls that Hoople was a quiet person who rarely spoke out publicly.[85] Later, in the debate in the legislature, Michael Cassidy of the NDP remembered Hoople: "[There was] a nice little old lady named Elizabeth Hoople. She got up to tell the Premier that … 'In the past … I voted for you, Mr. Premier, because I trusted you to maintain our democratic heritage. I now doubt it. You never came to Streetsville and you didn't call…. If you make a promise to discuss something, I want that someone to keep that promise.'" NDP Leader Stephen Lewis, no stranger to dramatic statements, interjected: "May Mrs. Hoople's name go down in the pages of history! That was the beginning of the end when Lizzy Hoople changed her mind!"[86]

In a letter to the editor later that year, Hoople explained why she felt loyal to her adopted town: "When I first came to Streetsville,

---

* The parkway belts through Mississauga were in fact very narrow, much narrower than what MTARTS or the *Toronto-Centred Region* plan had envisioned (albeit in less precise terms). Even so, the provincial government found itself under tremendous pressure from landowners who demanded generous compensation for this "downzoning." In mid-August, Davis wrote to the MPPs from the affected municipalities: "As you know, there are some conflicts between existing plans of major land users and the Parkway Belt proposals. As these must be resolved as soon as possible, I would appreciate it if you could serve on a special group set up for that purpose" (August 15, 1973—Archives of Ontario, RG 3-49, tb 38, Davis General Correspondence, 1973).

over forty years ago, it was still a small village, but it didn't take me long to realize that there was something special and different about it. It was the collective spirit of the place. Streetsville was a town with a heart, a good strong kindly heart that steadily through the years had cared for its citizens, welding them together and creating in them a pride in their town."[87]

Ron Farrow has vivid recollections of the Davis meeting, which he attended with the premier: "Here was this scene after it was all over ... Hazel simply looked up at the premier and said, 'Well, Bill?'... and he looked down at Hazel and said 'Sorry, Hazel.' And that was it. It was over. Done. He'd gone out, faced the music, and stuck to his guns."

The legislative assembly's deliberations on Bill 138 were not lengthy. Several hours were spent on second reading, and there was a late-night Committee of the Whole session followed by third and final reading. The opposition members devoted most of their attention to the Streetsville issue. The most outspoken MPP in the debate was Ottawa's Michael Cassidy. He argued that proceeding with Peel-only and Halton-only regional governments amounted to a repudiation of the *Toronto-Centred Region* plan. He also believed that Burlington belonged with the Hamilton region, not with Halton.

Despite exhortations by the speaker of the assembly to confine himself "to the principle of the bill,"[88] Cassidy alleged that Davis favoured Bill 138 because land developers did, and that Mississauga politics was dominated by land developers. He accused Mayor Chic Murray of being a "bagman" for both the Conservatives and the developers. Cassidy also sought assurances that Lou Parsons would not be appointed chairman of the new region. He claimed that, after the death of Mayor Robert Speck, Parsons had been appointed "the reeve [of Mississauga] over the then-deputy reeve [Grant Clarkson] because the then-deputy reeve was being a bit uncomfortable for the powers that be."[89]

The member for Peel South, Doug Kennedy, brother of Mississauga Councillor Harold Kennedy and a nephew of a late former premier (T.L. Kennedy), was infuriated by these attacks: "I'm concerned about the allegations the honourable member has made against honourable members of the local municipality; men of integrity who have served the municipality well. He makes allegations against them and smears their characters."[90]

Kennedy had lived in Streetsville for a few years after World War II. "I have nothing but pleasant memories of Streetsville," he says, looking back. "It was idyllic. Elections were exciting." The former MPP adds, however, that he was convinced that the arguments for three, as opposed to four, lower-tier municipalities were valid.[91]

Davis appeared in the assembly when debate entered Committee of the Whole stage. With Parsons and Peel Warden Ivor McMullin looking on, the premier defended his program:

> I am not saying for a moment the e isn't some logic to the arguments of the town of Streetsville and the citizens there, heaven knows. I also say with respect, Mr. Chairman, it is just as difficult for us to make a determination that does upset a number of people in Streetsville as it would be to accede to their request, believing it, perhaps, in the long run not to be in the interests of the total community.[92]

On justifying Halton and Peel as separate regions:

> I'm not saying it reflects the unanimous opinion of everybody in the county of Peel or Halton necessarily, but the desire to have a single [upper tier] unit within Peel, I think, is relatively well supported as a matter of principle and I believe this to be true in Halton.[93]

On June 29, 1973, it was all over. The bill received Royal Assent. Only six months remained in Streetsville's life as a municipality. Administrative and technical preparations for the restructuring were already underway.

Areas of Regional and Local Jurisdiction as Envisioned by the Province in 1973

REGIONAL

Regional Planning
Land Division Committee
Water Supply and Distribution
Sanitary Sewers and
Sewage Treatment
Regional Storm Sewers
(*e.g. along regional roads*)
Garbage Disposal
Regional Roads
Regional Parking
Traffic Control
Public Transit (Optional)
Police Protection
Heath and Welfare
Licensing (eg. salvage yards)
Homes for the Aged
County Forests
Conservation Appointments
Industrial Development
Emergency Measures
Capital Borrowing
Museums

LOCAL

Local Planning
Subdivision Agreements
Committee of Adjustment
Local Storm Sewers
(*e.g. along local roads*)

Public Transit
Garbage Collection
Local Roads
Local Parking
Local Parks
Fire Protection
Recreation
Building Inspection
Building Permits
Animal Control
Tax Collection
Libraries
Licensing

PART II
Leaving a Legacy

The Land
of Bread
and Honey

4

Saturday, June 2, 1973, was a big day for Streetsville. On that weekend in the late spring, under a brilliant, warm sun, many local residents and visitors turned out for the first annual Streetsville Founder's Bread and Honey Festival.

"Streetsville should certainly be proud," the *Review* subsequently commented. "The whole [event] was a resounding success."[1]

Between 4,000 and 15,000 people—estimates vary significantly—attended the carnival-like festivities in Memorial Park, and numerous others participated in the associated events, including the parade and the Miss Streetsville pageant.

Part of Memorial Park resembled a fort. Attendees were greeted by a meticulously uniformed sentry from the Royal Regiment of Canada. These troops were joined by representatives of the Six Nations Reserve near Brantford, who put together an elaborate showcase of traditional Iroquois culture. Also on hand were members of the Upper Canada Rifles, decked out in their buckskin and coon caps. At appointed times throughout the day, they put on dis-

The community parade was one of the highlights of the first Streetsville Bread and Honey Festival. *Photographs courtesy of Paul McCallion (family album).**

* The photographs are in an album with unlabelled pictures from both the 1973 and 1974 festivals. It is possible, therefore, that they were taken at the second annual festival. The photographs were probably taken by Sam McCallion, although the photographer's name was not indicated.

plays with flintlock rifles and demonstrated the arts of knife- and axe-throwing. Meanwhile, visitors could quell their tastebuds with free bread and honey, courtesy of the local mills. The bread was baked on a brick oven constructed especially for the occasion. Most of the bricks were about 60 years old, as these were deemed to be especially well-suited for the purpose at hand.

If the sun became overbearing, the arena building had a "Gallery of Crafts" waiting to be enjoyed. Many visitors did not leave empty-handed, as the selection was impressive. Numerous prints by highly regarded local artist Ted Ledsham were displayed, as was a variety of pottery, ceramics, and jewellery.

Because the pedestrian bridge to "The Island" had not yet been constructed, a temporary dike was created for the occasion. The Island was the site of the Rotary Beer Tent, which would develop a somewhat dubious reputation. Following the second festival, a lengthy discussion ensued about what to do with the beer tent, remembers Jim Guest, who has volunteered every year. "Crowd control was a problem. Only 300 people would be allowed into the tent. There were problems with people trying to pass booze under the tent [to others]." Guest recalls that concerns also arose when some people—sober or otherwise—tried to swim across the river to the mainland. Fortunately, there were no injuries.[2]

The noon hour marked the official close of the fishing derby. The event, open only to young people aged 16 years and under, was organized by the Kinsmen Club. Members had stocked the Credit River with about 300 trout. The derby proved to be enormously popular, and organizers regretted not having more fish, recalls Al Macdonald, one of the Kinsmen volunteers.[3]

The Kinsmen were kept occupied on other fronts. That evening they had to be ready to host the Founder's Ball in the arena building, between 9 p.m. and 1 a.m. Those attending were requested to honour the occasion by wearing period costume.[4] Organizers could not have asked for better attendance; more than 640 people purchased tickets, which sold for eight dollars per couple. The Jack Denton Orchestra of "Palais Royale and Old Mill fame" provided entertainment, and proceeds from the evening went to cystic fibrosis research.[5]

The highlight of Bread and Honey weekend was organized by Frank Haddon, Streetsville's resident parade marshal and a descendant of Timothy Street. Haddon had previously put together about a dozen parades for various community celebrations. "Organizing parades is something he loved to do and he did it well," recalls the late co-ordinator's wife, Claudia.[6] "He was simply great at it," affirms Al Betts, who headed the Streetsville and District Chamber of Commerce. "We were so impressed at how he was able to pull together all the groups."[7]

On Saturday afternoon, beginning at 1:30 p.m., the big parade slowly proceeded south on Queen Street toward the arena. The marshalling grounds were on Britannia Road, just west of Queen. Seven bands, ranging from local school groups to the Brampton Senators Band, were featured. In addition, many organizations and businesses devoted considerable time to the construction of floats—15 in all. The Streetsville Senior Citizens' Club, for example, came riding down Queen Street in a float resembling the interior of an old country house. The members, who were dressed in 19th-century costumes, showcased some of their group's social and charitable activities.

Members of the Royal Canadian Legion proudly marched down the street, followed by a series of antique cars and tractors. Frank Dowling, Streetsville's first mayor and an old-car enthusiast, rode in his 1931 Ford Model A.

Ellen Dimitroff had only a few hours to prepare for the parade. On Friday, June 1, promptly at 8 p.m., the Miss Streetsville Pageant and Variety Night got underway at the Community Hall. Two dozen competitors vied for the crown. The event was sponsored by the chamber of commerce and overseen by Caye Killaby, a former Mississauga town councillor (and a candidate for Mississauga city council later that year) who resided near Streetsville. At about 10 p.m., Ellen Dimitroff had her coronation. Runners-up were Elaine Dadd and Mary Anne Kalapaca. Dimitroff thereby earned the privilege of being chauffeured down Queen Street the next morning in an open vehicle.

The first Streetsville Founder's Bread and Honey Festival had its glitches: the odd microphone that would not work, occasional extended gaps between parade floats, some delays getting the bread and honey ready, and of course the difficulties with the beer tent. In general, however, an enjoyable day was had by the townsfolk of Streetsville and those who joined them for what would, in future years, become the biggest event in the City of Mississauga and a popular annual Streetsville reunion.

Not surprisingly, it was not far from the minds of many residents that this might be the last big party for Streetsville as a municipality. The town's bid for a plebiscite on its future had failed, the cabinet had rejected its petition, and just days earlier the bill to put amalgamation into effect as of January 1, 1974, had been introduced at Queen's Park.

These political realities were not lost on the *Streetsville Review*. The paper ran an advertisement urging citizens "to wear black arm bands to mourn the death of Streetsville."[8] Few people heeded the call, however. "The first festival was definitely a celebration, not a funeral," remembers Sylvia Weylie, one of the key organizers and wife of the reeve.[9]

THE DISCUSSIONS AND PREPARATIONS

It was a celebration that almost did not happen. At its January 1973 meeting, the Streetsville Historical Society brainstormed how it could get involved, all the while uncertain about whether the big day would materialize.[10] At its March meeting, the Streetsville Public

Library Board was not sure that there would be a festival when it discussed whether to ask Mary Manning to prepare an updated version of *A Village Library*, which she had co-authored in 1959 with the Reverend T.D. Jones, formerly of Streetsville United Church.[11]

Many people in Streetsville today insist that the Bread and Honey Festival was to be a one-time event to say farewell to the town. This is not quite accurate. Although some residents may have attended the festival for these sentimental reasons, an examination of the Minutes and other documents describing the early discussions and planning meetings reveals that this was to be an annual event to perpetuate the vibrancy and community spirit in Streetsville, regardless of developments on the political front. Discussions about some sort of yearly festival commenced before amalgamation became a *fait accompli*.

In January 1972, shortly after the municipal elections, Councillor Peter Wright (Ward 3) was appointed to chair the Streetsville Promotional Committee, which would report to council's General Committee 1. Following a meeting on February 21, 1972, Wright announced that his committee had identified three priority areas: to investigate the proposal by the chamber of commerce for a Streetsville logo, develop an information brochure on the town, and "research the possibility of developing a festival."[12]

During the next several months, progress on all three fronts was slow. However, George Jacques of the Lions Club and Al Macdonald of the Kinsmen Club were appointed to the committee in August. Their participation and the efforts of others who joined in the subsequent months would be important to the development of a festival.

Shortly after that August report was presented, Wright resigned his seat on council because his employer was transferring him to Camden, New Jersey. Deputy Reeve Jim Graham, who was already chairing General Committee 1, assumed the leadership of the promotional committee.

Graham describes himself as an "ideas person."[13] His energy and creativity were well known to his fellow councillors. As expected, he assumed this new duty with enthusiasm, moving expeditiously on all three priority areas. When the committee met on September 13, 1972, the festival was no longer on the backburner.

A thorough proposal for the festivities had yet to be fully developed. However, the consensus which emerged from the meeting was that "the Town should hold an annual celebration in the form of a Carnival possibly at the end of January or beginning of February with all service organizations taking part." Members believed that a winter event would breathe life into the community during a slower time of the year. Besides, it was thought, Streetsville already had events in the spring, summer, and fall, including water races on the Credit River, a bicycle rodeo, a Lions Club concert, the Lions Jamboree, the Kinsmen June Dance, the Turkey Shoot at Memorial Park, and the Chamber of Commerce Trade Fair (held on alternate years). The only winter events of any note took place during the Christmas season, including the Policemen's Ball and the firefighters' annual Santa Claus festivities.

After some further discussion, the committee, on a motion by Al Macdonald, requested that Mayor McCallion "declare the first Saturday in February 1973, as the First Annual Streetsville Founders' Day." The motion also called for a special public meeting on October 4, 1972, "to propose projects and events for the day, which is a day of celebration honouring the founders of the Town of Streetsville."

By the time that meeting was called to order, doubts had been expressed about holding the event in the dead of winter. The objections were not difficult to anticipate: It might be too cold in early February, some were quick to point out; others asked what would happen if there was no snow on the appointed day; some attendees opined that it would be next to impossible to hold any kind of lively outdoor celebration such as a parade or concert.

Realizing that the consensus was breaking down, Jim Graham volunteered to do some homework. He spoke with—and in some cases visited—organizers of festivals in other parts of the province, including the Kleinburg Binder Twine Festival and the Elmira Maple Syrup Festival.* He wanted to investigate what made these events renowned and successful.

Graham was convinced that although it would be unrealistic to expect an enormously extravagant event the first year—resources are often hard to come by before there is a track record of success— the festival should ultimately aim for an attendance of about 40,000, which would permit it to be self-sustaining. He also surmised that the event could not simply be called the Streetsville Founders' Festival. "We needed a catch," he recalls.

When the promotional committee met on December 14, it had a clearer picture of what needed to be done. It was agreed that the proposal for a February event would be discarded and that the first weekend in June would be looked at instead. Graham was confident that the new time of year would be the most appropriate; he had consulted with provincial tourism officials who recommended that Streetsville should hold a major event in the spring, because most community festivals in Ontario took place in the fall. Graham also remembers that the committee had done some meteorological research which revealed that fair weather was more

---

* The annual Elmira event was launched in 1965 with the specific goal of promoting community spirit. Kleinburg's festival was revived in 1967, after a hiatus of nearly 40 years. Both events received considerable acclaim throughout the province. The festivals were drawing tens of thousands of visitors and mobilizing hundreds of volunteers and dozens of local groups, businesses, artists, craftspeople, and entertainers—while maintaining a small-town feeling.

probable on that weekend than on any other in spring.

The draft agenda for the festivities, drawn up by the committee at the December 14 meeting, was very similar to the one that was eventually implemented. Members also resolved that the theme would be "the use of flour," and they asserted that "this seems appropriate because the Town originated on a mill site and two mills still operate (flourish) near the southern boundary of the Town."[14]

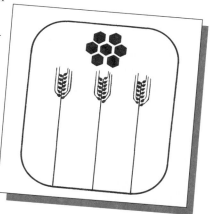

The festival logo

It would be early 1973 before the committee came up with an official name for the festival (one that garnered unanimous approval): "Bread and Honey Festival." The bread would represent the town's milling heritage, and honey had likewise been an important product in Streetsville and environs.[15]

Committee members also wished to honour the town's pioneering spirit. The word "Founder's"—which had already been used unofficially—was retained. Although the September 1972 resolution had intended that the festival honour "the founders of Streetsville," the first festival used the singular expression, "Streetsville *Founder's* Bread and Honey Festival." A promotional pamphlet explained that, "The main objective [is to] involve the entire Community in a fun filled day in honour of our Founder, Timothy Street." More recent festivals, however, have consistently used the plural, "Founders'."[16]

It had been hard enough to come up with the festival's format and theme. Executing the plan would prove to be much more challenging. Fortunately, many residents and community leaders were genuinely interested. The parks and recreation board was forthcoming in offering Memorial Park for the weekend, and the arena board also responded enthusiastically to a request to make its premises available.[17] Much to everyone's satisfaction, it did not take much to convince Frank Haddon to oversee the parade.

Some organizations were initially less receptive. Jim Graham recalls that it was difficult at first to convince the business community that this festival had the potential to greatly benefit the town—including retailers. Finally, in late March, the chamber of commerce agreed to accept the formal responsibility for administering the festival, and it received a grant of $1,000 from town council.[18] The chamber's decision came just in time. On March 21, the *Review* was still reporting that, "If the [Promotional] Committee could not find some person or group to take charge of the Bread and Honey Festival ... the said Festival would have to be cancelled."[19]

Before the chamber of commerce officially came on board, the promotional committee had already approached one of the chamber's most active members and its past president—Sam McCallion. The committee believed that McCallion could play an important role in making the festival a success. With the *Streetsville Booster,* he had at his disposal an important marketing tool. He did not disappoint; his coverage that year and every subsequent year was extensive. "Streetsville will be a beehive of activity" were almost always the famous first words. McCallion's connections with the local business community could help to bring much-needed support from that sector, and, because the nature of his business was such that local people were regularly calling him, he could serve as an excellent contact person for public enquiries, especially during working hours when other committee members were harder to reach. The fact he was the husband of the mayor could not have hurt much, either.

McCallion agreed to play an active part in the festival, and he continued to do so for many years. When the festival became an incorporated non-profit organization (in 1974), he was listed as its founding president. It would be 1982 before he bowed out of the leadership role.

Soon after the chamber of commerce took over the administration of the 1973 festival, several businesspeople came forward to offer their time and services. Among them were Gord Bentley, the deputy fire chief whose family owned the Bentley Hardware Store, and Ted Russell, the manager of the BP Gas Station who worked especially hard during the week before the festival to set up the grounds. Russell remembers that organizers were very detailed about the physical layout and put in a great deal of time making sure it would be as safe as possible.[20]

Although the chamber of commerce assumed responsibility for the first festival, many volunteers were not directly affiliated with that group. Jim Graham stayed involved, spending a great deal of his free time trying to recruit the various performers. He was joined by Reeve Bob Weylie, who put his organizational skills to good use as "festival manager", making sure that all the attractions were in place. When the incorporation papers were issued, Weylie and Graham were listed with McCallion as the founding directors.

Other local organizations quickly jumped on board. The service clubs worked tirelessly during the six to seven weeks preceding the event. Many members of Streetsville's Portuguese community likewise devoted their time, especially to the construction of the large brick oven in Memorial Park; Joe Simoes was in frequent consultation with other festival organizers.

The Streetsville Public Library decided to hold a concurrent book sale. Mary Manning, meanwhile, was kept busy writing *A History of Streetsville*, a short book released at the festival by the historical society. Demand was high, and subsequent editions were issued in 1976 and 1990. (Manning's updated history of the library, *A Village Library Grows*, was not published until later in 1973.)

*   *   *

As the final note was being struck at the Founder's Ball on that clear June night, some volunteers stood outside on the dimly lit lawn just beyond the arena parking lot. The Bread and Honey Festival had been worth the effort, they concurred, and it should continue. Those volunteers were founders in their own right, for their festival lives on. You can count on the fact that every year on the first weekend in June, Streetsville—as Sam McCallion so often put it—"will be a beehive of activity."

5 | Revitalizing Downtown Streetsville

Many visitors to Streetsville are impressed with its historic, charming downtown. But the now-appealing town core was once considerably less attractive.

In the late 1960s and early 1970s, parts of the downtown were deteriorating. There were several unsightly, vacant lots. Some of the old buildings looked drab. It was not uncommon to see storefronts with peeling paint. Most alleyways did not cater to pedestrian traffic. Sidewalks were merely standard, if not substandard. There were still overhead wires, signage was cluttered, and the several neon signs certainly commanded attention, but they seemed awkwardly out of place.

In the dying days of its life as a municipal entity, Streetsville confronted the challenges of downtown rehabilitation. The issue had been talked about, on and off, for several years. In a 1966 presentation to the Streetsville and District Chamber of Commerce, Peter Langer, executive vice president of Markborough Properties, argued that a committee to work on downtown renewal was urgently needed,[1] although no developers appear to have subsequently played a prominent role. In 1968, the chamber of commerce tried unsuccessfully to get some federal funds for this purpose, expressing urgency about the growing parking problem in the commercial area. A joint meeting of town council and core-area merchants on April 10, 1968, brought the inadequate parking situation and other issues, such as overhanging wires, to the forefront.[2] Although a committee was subsequently struck to address these matters, significant headway was not made.

The council which took the oath of office in January 1972 was determined to finally address the downtown issue in a concerted and noticeable way. Indeed, the subject received prominent airing in Hazel McCallion's speech that month, marking the commencement of her second term of office as mayor. Her Worship's important policy statement of December 1972 (discussed in Chapter 1) also underlined this priority. By then, council's interest had been bolstered by the work of architect Sergio Tarantino, who had received a joint federal-provincial grant to come up with concrete recommendations. His proposals included everything from extending the commercial zone down Main Street toward the Credit River to building an amphitheatre behind the town hall.[3] Meanwhile, local artist Wilfred Gelder drew up plans for an exciting town square around the highly visible brick cenotaph, which was situated in the middle of Main Street, just east of Queen.[4] (The cenotaph had been constructed in 1926 to honour 16 young men from Streetsville who did not return from World War I. Eight names were added after World War II.[5]) A committee of merchants was established to study the options, and, as a result, a few small steps were taken. In the late summer of that year, the town blocked some work being done by Bell Canada, insisting that all wiring should henceforth be underground.[6]

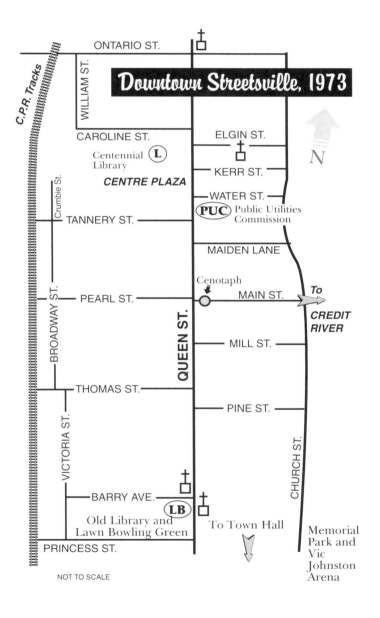

Downtown Streetsville, 1973

CPR Tracks

ONTARIO ST.

WILLIAM ST.

CAROLINE ST.

ELGIN ST.

KERR ST.

WATER ST.

Centennial (L) Library

CENTRE PLAZA

Crumbie St.

TANNERY ST.

PUC Public Utilities Commission

MAIDEN LANE

Cenotaph

PEARL ST.

MAIN ST.

To CREDIT RIVER

BROADWAY ST.

QUEEN ST.

MILL ST.

THOMAS ST.

VICTORIA ST.

PINE ST.

CHURCH ST.

BARRY AVE.

LB

Old Library and Lawn Bowling Green

To Town Hall

Memorial Park and Vic Johnston Arena

PRINCESS ST.

NOT TO SCALE

N

Still, the pace was slow, and the ideas were not formulated as coherently and precisely as they could have been. Some of Tarantino's recommendations, such as those calling for the construction of parking garages, simply did not resonate with the business community or the public.

"It was awfully hard to make changes," remembers the parks and recreation board's Ralph Hunter, a local insurance broker. Hunter notes that some property owners in the commercial area were not local residents.

A typical Streetsville storefront in the early 1970s. The town was determined to make its historic downtown brighter and more appealing. *Photograph courtesy of Doug Flowers.*

As long as they could keep their tenants, these landlords may have seen only the costs, and not the potential long-term benefits, of a concerted downtown improvement initiative.[7]

"Absentee landlords are a fact of life," concurs longtime local clothier and downtown property owner Eric Ladner, who estimates that at least 50 percent of the landlords did not reside in town. "They're people who invest in a community and buy a building, and then they rent it out and take revenue from it. Sometimes there isn't any extra revenue from the building to upgrade it. Sometimes they don't have the desire to do it. Sometimes they don't have the knowledge or ambition to do it." Ladner adds, however, that "when the people who do own their buildings take the initiative and they set a standard ... then [absentee landlords] feel they have to get on the bandwagon [because] the buildings are getting run down and not too attractive, they lose their ability to rent, and they have a reputation for being landlords who have no interest except the revenue."[8]

"CORE '73"

In early 1973, Streetsville got lucky. Four University of Waterloo students, studying in different disciplines related to urban planning, were working on an academic assignment which required them to select a community and to determine, very specifically, how it could be beautified, refurbished, or redesigned to make it more vibrant for residents and economically viable for merchants. They chose Streetsville.

At a special meeting on January 25, 1973, the students—Doug Flowers, Miles Cullum, Peter Mah, and Derryk Renton—presented the results of their work. "We want Streetsville to have a purpose," remarked Flowers, who grew up just outside the town's boundaries and who served as the group's facilitator. The meeting featured slides of some downtown properties, followed by artist's renditions showing how even small enhancements could make all the difference. In some cases, a simple coat of paint could go a long way. Flowers, who was working on a Master's degree, noted that what was needed was downtown rehabilitation and not redevelopment. Demolitions, massive overhauls, and major new construction projects were not in the equation. The key was to showcase and improve what already existed. Even where significant, long-term changes were envisioned, they were intended to ensure the preservation or restoration of Streetsville's friendly, traditional, small-town atmosphere. Flowers added that the town had the very real potential to cultivate a market for tourism.[9]

The response from the merchants, the politicians, and the press was positive. The *Mississauga Times* observed that,

The above photograph shows the Montreal House at Queen and Pearl Streets as it looked in 1973. The other photograph is of a sketch prepared by the Core '73 team showing how modest upgrades could make this commercial property more attractive. *Photographs courtesy of Doug Flowers.*

Above all the cost of the transformation would not be prohibitive. The refurbishing scheme is … both attractive and realistic. The committee's resolve to obtain Opportunities for Youth funds and a municipal grant in the face of extinction via regional government shows the town does not need a big brother to plan its destiny.

Perhaps the province's rule by flow chart is workable but will it engender the enthusiasm shown for the core revitalization?[10]

The merchants' steering committee, led by Eric Ladner, recommended that town council allocate up to $15,000 to finance various aspects of the rehabilitation and that the students be employed from April until September. The Waterloo group, for its part, applied for and received a federal grant amounting to $5,500.[11] The improvements to public property that were undertaken in 1973 were, of course, paid for by the municipality. For example, $42,500 was allocated for installing interlocking brick sidewalks.[12]

Councillor Jim Watkins, a local chiropractor, was delegated to oversee the project. At Streetsville's final town council meeting, on December 31, 1973, he would comment that the completion of Phase One of the downtown rehabilitation program was perhaps council's most significant recent achievement.[13]

The group quickly defined its first principles. The students strongly believed that downtown rehabilitation was not merely an exercise in making roads, buildings, and sidewalks more pleasant to the human eye, but that the way communities were designed and maintained had important social and political implications. Many post-World War II urban and suburban developments were, they opined, dehumanizing. "To make way for the automobile, we built massive road and freeway networks," the final report stated. "The result was the placing of individuals into their own sound-proof cars and away from personal interactions. The result was also the breaking up of any pedestrian atmosphere which may have existed. The meeting and talking function was totally disrupted in a physical sense."[14]

The sidewalk in this shot of Queen Street during the summer of 1973 has been ripped out to prepare for the placement of interlocking bricks. *Photograph courtesy of Doug Flowers.*

That same year, for instance, construction was completed on the 1.5-million-square-foot Square One Shopping Centre in central Mississauga, under the auspices of S.B. McLaughlin and Associates. According to the Core '73 group, Streetsville had to act immediately to avoid the fate of other towns: "If the difference between Metropolitan Toronto's problems and Streetsville's is largely one of scale, then surely we should act as soon as possible to guide the [rehabilitation] of the downtown."[15]

To create a unique atmosphere in Streetsville, it was proposed that the community adhere to a traditional, late-19th-century theme. In view of the financial constraints on the retailers, however, the Core '73 group acknowledged that enhancements would have to be in the range of $500 to $2,000 per merchant. The students continued to insist that even modest investments could go a long way.

One obvious target was the community's messy and tacky signage. Third-party advertising and neon signs would have to go. Only signs identifying a local business and municipal signs could remain.

The local streets and sidewalks were also badly in need of improvement. Queen Street, for example, had many potholes, and the adjacent sidewalks required fixing. Thomas Street was even worse. Although Queen and Thomas were county roads, Peel finally did commence work on some long-awaited improvements. Sidewalks were under the town's jurisdiction, and it was soon agreed that Streetsville would be used as a test site—among the first in Canada—for interlocking brick sidewalks, which are now, of course, much more common. The bricks were purchased from Durastone, a Mississauga company. Work began in early July 1973 and continued through much of the summer.[16]

The core needed more foliage. Tree-planting along Queen Street thus became another priority, and the students often directly pitched in. It was a painstaking task because of the existing underground service wires and gas mains. The work had to be carefully orchestrated with the town, the public utilities commission, the County of Peel, Bell Canada, Ontario Hydro, and Consumers Gas. A co-ordinating committee, consisting of representatives of these stakeholders, was chaired by Streetsville's public works director, Keith Cowan. Technical details included:

- Underground wiring of light standards required protective insulation to prevent interference with gas mains.

- Co-ordination to ensure that the Core '73 construction and Bell Canada's work on reinforcing ducts on Queen Street would not conflict.

- Old telephone poles, already slated for removal, would have to remain for several months longer. "This probably means that these old poles will exist for a while after the new sidewalks are constructed, and that they will have to be removed later," read the Minutes of the June 29, 1973, meeting. "Some special technique will have to be employed in removing these poles so that the new sidewalks will not be spoiled." The committee went on to conclude that the holes could be filled by a weak concrete mix, an asphalt mix, or tamped gravel.

• Selection and acquisition of the new lights. (Tri-globe lights were eventually picked.)[17]

An important legacy of Core '73 was the initiation of the Streetsville Core Development Association, a body of merchants charged with promoting and carrying on the rejuvenation of the downtown well after the students had moved on to other endeavours. Although Streetsville already had a longstanding chamber of commerce, it was agreed that the interests and aspirations of the downtown merchants were sufficiently distinct to warrant a new organization. Looking back, Peter Mah says that the fledgling SCDA ended up playing an essential role. "If it wasn't for that association, we would not have been able to muster the enthusiasm from the merchants," he remarks.

Mah adds that political backing was also crucial. He recalls, for example, that the mayor came through with "amazing" support and that the council was "very focussed and determined."[18]

The SCDA was the forerunner to the Streetsville Business Improvement Area (BIA), which was established in 1980. The students themselves recommended that a BIA be established. Ontario's first BIA, Toronto's Bloor West Village, had been launched in 1970 and was already proving to be a success. Municipalities are authorized to set up such districts, usually after canvassing (or having received a petition from) area businesses.[19] Once a BIA is launched, all property owners, merchants, and other businesspeople in the designated zone must join. A special levy is collected from these members. The funds are used for local beautification, marketing, and the co-ordination of events and activities which improve the area's economic viability.

By mid-year, much of the business community was on board with the Core '73 projects.[20] That fall, the team was sounding very encouraged. "When they have seen these plazas going up [such as Square One], some of them assumed a defeatist attitude instead of fighting back," Flowers told the *Mississauga News*. "We have had to work against this and I'm happy to say that the trend has reversed and [the merchants] are all encouraged.

"We've got a commitment from 50 percent of the merchants already that they plan to do something to their stores. Ten to fifteen percent have already done something and I think we will be twenty percent completed by Christmas. We're like a little steam engine chugging up a steep slope to the top of the hill."[21]

Although they were careful to emphasize their gradual, incremental approach to downtown renewal, the Core '73 group was cognizant that the commercial environment in Streetsville would have to undergo a  more significant change over time. Streetsville could never hope to compete with the malls and large retailers on their own terms. The town's hardware stores, shoe stores, and non-specialized clothing outlets might find the competition increasingly prohibitive. Streetsville did have three antique stores, but more such businesses would be needed in order for the community to acquire a commercial identity. The artisans, pottery makers, sculptors, and proprietors of rare collectibles would have to be attracted to the town.

With characteristic enthusiasm, Core '73, which worked out of a small office at 249 Queen Street South, put out a general letter to dozens of niche merchants who had small outlets or boutiques in other communities. "We would like to suggest," the group wrote, "that Streetsville can offer the relaxing, people-oriented atmosphere which is so necessary to the success of an independent, craft producing operation, and yet still be within 25 miles of the Toronto market and at the centre of the growing Mississauga market. Furthermore, a number of buildings suitable for retail and/or studio purposes are presently available."[22]

Although some interest was apparently generated, the group, in its final report, conceded that the letter to niche businesses was premature. The students now concluded that the revitalization must proceed first. It was hoped that the small-scale entrepreneurs would notice the results and gravitate to Streetsville.[23]

A VISION FOR THE FUTURE

Core '73 likewise left Streetsville with a clear vision of how the downtown could look in several years. The students called for an area which was highly pedestrian-oriented; they even contemplated closing off much of Queen Street to vehicles, or at least building wider sidewalks and permitting no on-street parking (additional lots would be constructed behind buildings). Mill Street, Ontario Street, and Main Street would be partly commercial "special policy areas" with good connections to the Credit Valley, especially for pedestrians and cyclists.[24]

The cenotaph would be the focal point for a new town square. The southern half of Main Street, between Queen Street and Church Street, would be closed to vehicular traffic. It would have trees, benches, and public washrooms.

Some of the recommendations for future downtown renewal might have caused difficulties had they been implemented. One proposal called for opening Church Street to commercial activity, while making it and Queen Street one-way. Most downtown areas which have implemented one-way traffic systems find them less, not more, pedestrian-oriented; they encourage faster, unobstructed traffic. Removing on-street parking would probably also have made the road more conducive to through vehicular circulation and could have cancelled an advantage which the Streetsville merchants already had over the malls—the shopper did not have to walk long distances (and through a large, bleak parking lot) to reach a store.

Although lessening the dominance of the automobile was an important and laudable objective, completely banning vehicles on Queen Street between Mill and Tannery Streets, which was identified as a long-term goal, might have precipitated unforeseen difficulties. An obvious one would have been parking. Because such a pedestrian mall would be designed to appeal to tourists, considerable automobile traffic to Streetsville would have to be expected. Where would the larger lots be constructed? Would they detract from the town's historic atmosphere? Would the extra outdoor walking keep some visitors away, especially on weekdays? The success of such a venture would probably have depended in part on the types of businesses in the pedestrian zone. Conventional merchants catering to day-to-day needs (clothing, hardware, shoes, or variety stores) would have suffered further, but if the area became wholly tourist-oriented (a Streetsville version of the *Rue du Trésor,* for example), the result could have been more promising. Even then, however, residents could have legitimately questioned whether they wished for their town to be a *de facto* theme park rather than a genuine, functional community.

These concerns notwithstanding, the new City of Mississauga would acquire a community which had reviewed its downtown renewal options carefully, taken some widely accepted steps to implement change, and largely won over the merchant community. The people of Streetsville hoped that the momentum would not be lost.

Electing the First City Council

6

L ate in the evening of Monday, October 1, 1973, a melancholy Chic Murray appeared at the Port Credit branch of the Royal Canadian Legion. The 59-year-old mayor of the Town of Mississauga mounted the podium to do what had been unthinkable just a short time earlier; he was conceding defeat to a 31-year-old candidate with no experience in elected office, Dr. Martin L. Dobkin.

Charles Myron Murray had led the Mississauga council since April 1972. He had been the town's reeve but accepted the mayor's chain of office following the death of Robert Speck, who survived only a few months after a risky heart transplant in late 1971. Murray had been Speck's closest political confidant, although he had a lower profile than his deceased predecessor had enjoyed. Whereas Speck had come across as charming and personable, Murray was perceived as very serious and sometimes aloof—the number cruncher behind the scenes.

This was the first election for Mississauga *city* council. Murray, with 15 years of experience in public office and an expensive, professional campaign, had entered the race confident that he would emerge as the mayor of the newly amalgamated city, which would now include Streetsville and Port Credit. Instead, he would remain off the stage during the January 1974 swearing-in ceremony.

Murray arrived to address his supporters a few hours after the last ballots had been cast, and with 96 percent of the polls reporting. A crowd of 500 gathered for what had been billed as a "victory celebration." Instead, the political veteran was trailing by 2,500 votes, a margin which would grow to 3,000 before the night was out.

Following his short speech, Murray made his way to T.L. Kennedy Secondary School, the traditional election-night gathering place in Mississauga, to formally concede defeat. Earlier that evening, the gymnasium had been packed with several hundred anxious candidates, campaign officials, and interested onlookers, witnessing (and experiencing) the suspense, elation, and dejection. By the time Murray arrived, only about a dozen election officials and reporters were left at the school,[1] which was named after the late prominent Peel MPP and one-time provincial premier.

Chic Murray was not, of course, the only candidate to concede defeat at T.L. Kennedy that night. A string of others had preceded him, many announcing that they would take a vacation to recuperate from the experience. Relieved that it was over, Murray promised that there would be no telephone at the family cottage.[2]

The 1973 election for Mississauga's first city council produced a remarkable result. Some seasoned incumbents and high-profile candidates had been turned aside by a frustrated electorate, disillusioned with what were perceived as fast-buck, poorly formulated, corporate-driven policies. Six of the 10 members of the new Mississauga council (Dobkin and councillors-elect Mary Helen Spence, Caye Killaby, David Culham, Hubert Wolf, and of course

Streetsville's Hazel McCallion) were described as "reformers." Although the reform candidates had not organized themselves into a formal electoral association, their platforms were, in many respects, congruent with Dobkin's. The mayoral challenger focussed on several critical themes: a reduction in the pace of development, especially high-density development; a large central park and more park space throughout the community; much-improved transit services; the need to severely limit, if not eliminate, the construction of strip plazas; citizen participation in all development and redevelopment planning; "adaptive" development, including an emphasis on preserving the environment; relocating the civic centre back to the Four Corners in Cooksville; and confining industrial operations to industrial parks. The reformers sometimes said that they wanted to see Mississauga grow to a maximum ultimate population of 500,000 to 750,000, rather than one million or more. They were infuriated that Mayor Murray and town officials were forecasting "greater incremental growth than ever experienced in the past,"[3] allegedly without adequate plans to deal with such growth.

Bruce McLaughlin, the flamboyant and widely recognized Mississauga-based developer, had become a poster boy for everything the reformers disliked about the development industry. A few years earlier, after Mississauga's town hall in Cooksville was partially destroyed by fire, the council and administration moved to a new building in what was then nothing but an empty field. It was a nondescript edifice at 1 City Centre Drive, which McLaughlin had given to the town in a land-swapping deal. The developer had great dreams of a new "city centre" on his still-vacant lands in central Mississauga, but he needed an anchor. The municipal offices would serve that purpose.

McLaughlin was well-read and astute. He was also a published author. A few months before the election, he released *100 Million*

Canadians: A Development Policy for Canada. As frightening as he seemed to many Mississaugans, McLaughlin was a visionary who, on paper at least, had some progressive ideas. He called for "easements which will accommodate transportation systems of the present and the future,"[4] and believed that, "Planning, rather than political influence or *laissez faire* economics, must protect the public interest so our communities can benefit from [the lessons revealed by] the mistakes which have occurred throughout urbanized areas in other parts of the world."[5] He argued that, "The only way to overcome urban sprawl is to restrict the culprits, whoever they may be and thus eliminate plug-in development."[6] He called for self-contained, multi-use, master-planned communities.

But McLaughlin's reputation suffered for several reasons: He enjoyed the spotlight and therefore became a lightning rod for all grievances against the development industry; his company alone owned virtually all the vacant lands in central Mississauga; he was perceived as dictating policy to the politicians; and many residents did not like what they had seen to that point, including the unattractive town hall which had been built in the middle of nowhere rather than in an established community like Cooksville. Hazel McCallion frequently charged that McLaughlin was trying to create an "artificial heart" for the city.

THE STREETSVILLE WARD

The first contender to bow to the winds of reform that election night by conceding his defeat was a candidate in Ward 9 (Streetsville). Grant Clarkson was Hazel McCallion's only challenger for the seat. He was trounced by a 76- to 24-percent margin.

Clarkson, 57, was not a political neophyte. He had a long and respectable track record in public office in the Township of Toronto and later the Town of Mississauga. A determined, dedicated conservationist, and a mechanical engineer by profession,

Clarkson grew up in the Dixie area, a descendant of one of the district's well-known pioneer families. One of his great grandfathers on his mother's side was Colonel Sam Price, a prominent 19th-century public figure in the Township of Toronto. Clarkson reflected often on his small-town roots, as he still does: "You probably haven't heard the way problems were solved in the old Dixie area, so let me tell you," he says, recalling a story told by Bruce Pallett. "When the Guthries had a problem, they took it to the Stanfields. When the Stanfields couldn't solve it, they went to the Palletts. And the Palletts couldn't solve the problem, so they went to the Clarksons. The Clarksons couldn't solve the problem, so they went to the Watsons. And the Watsons couldn't solve it, so they went to God.

"I had nowhere else to run," Clarkson says, reminiscing about the 1973 campaign.[7] He was on the losing end of a game of political musical chairs caused by the emergence of the new city. At the time of the election, Clarkson, a father of three who had moved to a sprawling farm on the Base Line in 1956, was reeve of the Town of Mississauga. Previously the deputy reeve, he was promoted by council when Lou Parsons, who had held the reeve's position, was named by the provincial government on July 31, 1973, to be the first chairman of the Regional Municipality of Peel. The Town of Mississauga, like the Town of Streetsville, had three officials elected at large: the mayor, reeve, and deputy reeve. For the new City of Mississauga, there would be a mayor and nine councillors—and two wards (8 and 9) were set aside for Streetsville and Port Credit.

This created the possibility that some incumbents would have to face other incumbents. The situation became somewhat less complicated when Parsons was removed from the equation and when Councillor Glenn Grice, to everyone's surprise, announced that he would not be seeking re-election. But this still did not address Clarkson's predicament.

Grant Clarkson, reeve of the Town of Mississauga, challenged Streetsville Mayor Hazel McCallion for a seat on the new Mississauga city council. *Photograph courtesy of Grant Clarkson.*

Clarkson apparently contemplated sitting out of the race. There was speculation that he would be appointed chairman of the Credit Valley Conservation Authority, where he had served faithfully as a Mississauga representative for the previous six years. (He later got this appointment anyway.)

The Mississauga reeve decided, however, to test his luck in Streetsville against the well-entrenched Hazel McCallion. Clarkson had some ties to Streetsville. He had served as chairman of the building committee of Streetsville United Church, and his home was only a short distance south of town. Clarkson had also expressed some sympathy for Streetsville's views; more so, perhaps, than his colleagues on Mississauga town council.[8] He had rolled up his sleeves for many charitable and civic initiatives in Peel County.

None of McCallion's counterparts on Streetsville's council seriously contemplated challenging the high-profile, popular mayor, who had a reputation for standing up for Streetsville. The town's politicians had, after all, demonstrated remarkable unity—indeed often unanimity—in 1973.

Many residents of Streetsville and the surrounding area were urging Reeve Robert Weylie to seek the Ward 4 seat on the new council. Ward 4 covered a large area, completely surrounding Streetsville. It was reported that Weylie was, in fact, seriously considering putting his name forward. He even left the business world to make more time for politics.[9] Weylie chose, however, to forego the opportunity. The eventual Ward 4 victor, Caye Killaby, a Mississauga town councillor from 1968 to 1970, had unsuccessfully challenged Chic Murray in 1970 for the post of reeve of the Town of Mississauga. She had polled 8,387 votes, about 1,300 fewer than Murray. A former head of the Mississauga Public Library Board, Killaby was often seen in Streetsville volunteering for one project or another. She had a reputation for being a community-minded reformer.

The 1973 contest for the Streetsville Ward was the first time a local election was held in Streetsville in which none of the candidates was a resident of the community. The McCallions lived just outside the town, on a farm on Britannia Road West in Mississauga, but they owned property in Streetsville—the little yellow industrial building at the corner of Alpha Mills Road and Falconer Drive, which was home to Unique Printing and the *Streetsville Booster*.

Clarkson believed that "the main difference" between the two Ward 9 candidates was the degree to which they could establish good relations with the other Mississauga politicians. Clarkson argued that he could offer "a better entrée, a better rapport with the people of Mississauga than Hazel has. It's a matter of fact that we're going to have regional government. We can't turn the clock back.

"There would have to be animosity [between McCallion and the other councillors]," Clarkson contended. "There's been a continual battle going on."[10] Earlier in the year, he had accused McCallion of being a "political warmonger" because she blamed the conservation authority for flooding along the Mullett Creek.[11]

In her campaign, McCallion disputed Clarkson's claims: "The co-operation is already proceeding since the day the decision was made by the province.... We must get on with the job of making the new City of Mississauga work for the whole city."[12]

The *Mississauga News* agreed with Clarkson, and it gave him—as well as Murray—strong editorial endorsements. The *Mississauga Times* sided with McCallion and Dobkin.

By mid-1973, McCallion was probably Peel's best-known municipal politician, and many Streetsville residents, as well as reformers in the Town of Mississauga, were urging her to run for mayor of the new city. Newspaper reports at the time suggested that she was seriously considering such a move. Martin Dobkin believes this is why the Streetsville mayor insisted on meeting him about a year before the vote (which would have been before Streetsville's fate was sealed): "I drove up to see Hazel one day, whom I had never met in my life. It was a cold, bitter, snowy day in November or December [1972]. I found the old town hall where her office used to be," he muses. "I went in, and she had heard I think by this time that I was going to run for mayor. She was quite upset and she wanted to meet me. She wanted to know who this idiot that was running for mayor that she'd never heard of before.

"So I went up there and I met her. The heating wasn't working in that part of the building and she also shared it with the police department.... We sat down and she was quite direct and gruff. She said to me, 'Well, who are you and what political experience do you have?' And I said 'none', and she said, 'Well, what are you running for mayor for?' I said, 'Well, I believe I have a good chance of winning.' And of course she had wanted to run herself. But I entered the picture. I don't know why, but she decided she would defer at the time and run for ward councillor. As I was leaving, she said, 'Well, you'd better win then!'"[13]

"No, I can't recall [pause]. No." This is McCallion's response when asked by the author if she considered running for mayor of Mississauga in the 1973 election. She does remember, however, having a meeting with Dobkin at some point before the election, at which time he stated his determination to challenge Murray.[14]

THE RACE FOR MAYOR

Dobkin, who notes that he knew he would run as early as the spring of 1972, officially declared his candidacy at the end of June 1973, just as the dust was settling on Bill 138. A family physician and county coroner, the challenger came out immediately with a platform which positioned him as a clear alternative to Murray. Whereas the latter was widely regarded as a promoter of fast growth and as a friend of the developers, Dobkin was not of the sort. Dobkin promptly issued his call for an end to high-rise development, demanded that a large, multi-use recreational park be created (a position which Murray himself later espoused in the campaign), promised to appoint a local ombudsman to ensure better scrutiny of the municipal administration, called for a written code of ethics for all municipal employees, insisted on strict spending limits for candidates in local elections, and said that Mississauga's beleaguered transit system—privately contracted to Charterways and fraught with problems[15]—needed to be completely overhauled. Dobkin mused that the Toronto Transit Commission should be approached to perform that role.[16]

Although he was relatively unknown, not particularly wealthy, and certainly short of wealthy friends, Dobkin gave some of the more seasoned pretenders to the mayoral throne something to worry about. Ron Searle, Ward 7 councillor and then deputy reeve of Mississauga following Clarkson's elevation to reeve, had been eyeing the top job. Searle apparently believed that he could unseat Murray in a contest with two major competitors. With three serious candidates, however, Murray might be able to come up the middle.[17]

Perhaps this, too, was Hazel McCallion's assessment. A race for mayor in 1973 might have been risky, putting her in danger of sitting out of politics for three years, watching her accomplishments fade into ever-more-distant memories. On the other hand, her victory in the Streetsville Ward was virtually guaranteed.[18]

The race for mayor did include two other candidates—both of whom were considered longshots. One was Eberhart Matuschka, who pledged to bring "common sense" to public office and to hold referenda on pressing public issues. But the most colourful challenger was Douglas Campbell, a perennial candidate with NDP ties, who called Murray's years of public service "15 years of incompetence." In fact, Campbell often played beautifully into Dobkin's hands. Take one of his statements at an all-candidates' meeting: "I think that this council has been here for two centuries too long, at least. I'm not sug-gesting that you vote for Campbell, [but] at least let's get rid of the Conservative [Murray] that we have here. You know, I'll settle for Dobkin. I like a few of his statements, but I'm not going to get car-ried away, you know—he's another member of the establishment.

"Let's take a look at Mr. Dobkin's brochure here," Campbell continued. "And take a look at the [slogan], 'Murder on Number 10 Highway!' I wholly concur with his statement. The 10 Highway area, from Burnhamthorpe to the Q.E. [Queen Elizabeth Way] is an abortion of planning and development. I'd like to know how many bodies that Mr. Murray carried off that road over the years."[19]

On the podium, Murray certainly came across as the most sea-soned candidate. Never at a loss for answers—and always quick to point out his experience as a politician and businessman—he could easily ad-lib. Dobkin had a more hesitant platform manner, although he was effective at answering questions and often drew applause as he condemned Murray's policies. He tended to give the same speech, however. He never memorized it, and his face was sometimes buried in his notes. Dobkin did, however, become sharper on his feet as the campaign progressed, and he never failed to tag Murray with a big money, big developer, Big Blue Machine label. Dobkin would often refer to his main opponent as "Mr. Appointed Mayor," because Murray had inherited the position from Robert Speck and had never actually faced the people for the

Chic Murray (left) and Martin Dobkin were the main contenders for the office of mayor of the new City of Mississauga. Murray was already mayor of the Town of Mississauga. Dobkin, a political neophyte, successfully challenged the veteran politician on a strongly pro-reform platform. *Photograph by Fred Loek,* Mississauga News. *Reprinted with the permission of the* Mississauga News.

post (although he was elected reeve in the 1970 general election).[20] Dobkin was given additional political mileage when labour troubles at Mississauga Hydro came to a head. The mayor, who was on the hydro commission, was now being trailed by angry striking employees of the municipal utility.

"How much are you spending on your campaign?" Dobkin would often demand rhetorically of Murray. "How much is McLaughlin giving you? He who pays the piper, plays the tune.

"We are being inundated with high-rise apartment ghettoes, shabby strip plazas and inadequate and dangerous roads. Subdivision after subdivision [is] being hastily thrown up with either absent or insufficient recreational facilities, and sorely lacking in functional parkland."

The good doctor went on to argue that high-rise apartments adversely affect the mental and physical health of those who live there. He decried the high concentration of apartments planned for—or already situated along—the Hurontario Street corridor. "This town is being choked to death by high-density development!" he exclaimed.[21]

Dobkin persistently called for "humanizing development, not dehumanizing development," but he and the other reform candidates for council sometimes appeared to regard all forms of high-density development as "dehumanizing." Even in Streetsville, the planning consultants who were conducting a review of the official plan reported in July 1973 that "it appears from public reaction at public meetings that people are generally very concerned about residential use other than single family homes."[22]

There were, of course, pockets of Mississauga which were becoming bleak apartment zones, but the reformers failed to take notice of the observations of some prominent critics of conventional planning, such as Jane Jacobs, who argued that multi-use, low-rise, mixed-income, *high-density* development was possible—even preferable to the rather stale, "expert-planned", often-uniform, low-density suburban landscape.[23] Moreover, the reformers' call for lower densities *and* better amenities, including a high-quality transit system, is rather difficult to reconcile. Indeed, the reform agenda sometimes revealed what might be labelled "the ambivalence of the middle class."[24] One can detect, often within the same pamphlet or speech, genuine, progressive social consciousness, as well as more exclusivist objectives which did not fully consider the needs of those with low incomes.

Murray was infuriated with Dobkin's accusations. He often referred to his challenger as "Mr. Appointed Coroner," and protested that "to listen to [Dobkin], you'd think we live in the worst town on earth—that our residents are stupid for living here and buying houses."[25]

Murray insisted that he did not know—or want to know— who contributed to his campaign, adding that he had budgeted

$18,747. He pointed out that donations would go into a campaign trust fund managed by respected Mississauga lawyer Les Pallett and that Pallett "could be disbarred" for any shady dealings.[26]

Dobkin was convinced that most incumbent Mississauga politicians were active members of the Conservative establishment in Peel. However, looking back now on his campaign, Dobkin contends that he was "too naïve" to notice the full extent of the Big Blue Machine's reach. He believes that belonging to that network was often a prerequisite for holding positions of influence and authority in Peel.

Murray frequently cited his considerable political experience, but was often taunted on this point by Dobkin: "If I had the fifteen years of experience the mayor says he has in his literature, I would be ashamed to put such experience in my literature—I wouldn't want anyone to know about it."[27]

Although Murray was usually more articulate than Dobkin, Murray's son Jim recalls that being the successor to the more charismatic Robert Speck was a hindrance to his father: "I think he had been in the shadow of a pretty dominant personality for a long, long time and was happy to be in that role; he was happy to work with Bob—they were very good friends. [But] I don't think it helped him."

Mayor Murray "had a strong belief that development was good for Mississauga, that it was a good source of revenue, that residential development and industrial development would feed on each other and that they would cross-pollinate and bring a good quality of life and bring amenities and maturity to the community," Jim Murray adds.[28]

As the combatants moved from venue to venue and as the enthusiasm and applause for Dobkin became more vigorous, Murray and his people had to know that the incumbent was facing a serious challenge. Fortunately for the mayor, his campaign team had the organization and resources to pull out all the stops. His canvassers called every household in Mississauga—often more than once. (Dobkin claims that he did not make any canvassing calls.) "Chic Murray" signs were plastered everywhere. Yet the slicker and more expensive Murray's campaign became, the more this appeared to the voters as confirmation of Dobkin's message that Murray was too close to the fast-buck developers.

Jim Murray insists, however, that despite the apparently growing receptiveness to Dobkin's candidacy, the mayor did not for a moment believe that his main challenger would emerge victorious: "My father had not the slightest idea that he was going to lose. However, during the election [campaign], it became obvious that there was a significant anti-development mood in some pockets. Did he think that there was [such a mood] prior to that? No. When Martin Dobkin was nominated, he thought he was a nuisance candidate."

The fact that Dobkin was young, as well as new to electoral politics, was highly appealing to many voters. "Have you ever seen a picture of him?" asks Streetsville's Bob Keeping, who had worked on the SPUR campaign and later helped Dobkin. "He looked so innocent. He was like the boy next door."[29]

The morning of election day, October 1, one of Murray's campaign co-chairs was still confidently predicting that his candidate's assertive campaigning would put him over the top—and with a two-to-one majority![30] Scarcely 12 hours later, he would be eating his words.

Only 28 percent of the 120,000 eligible voters actually bothered to come to the polls; low turnouts were the norm in municipal elections. Streetsville, as usual, showed the most democratic spirit; the voter turnout there was over 50 percent.[31] The turnout in Ward 8 (Port Credit) was higher than usual for that community, but still considerably lower than in Streetsville. Citizens in the lakeshore community were tired of the perceived incompetence and secrecy with which their town council had operated in its dying days. Ed Donner, a sitting member of the Port Credit council, was edged out by Hubert Wolf, a citizen activist and unabashed reformer. Wolf was no stranger to heated rhetoric. As chairman of the Port Credit Residents' Association, he had demanded a provincial investigation of the town's officials and complained to MPP Doug Kennedy that "Port Credit is an example of rape of the environment, an example of financial bungling which caused a fiasco in our tax structure. Too many high rises, overpopulation and wasteful, non vital road construction got us deep into debts."[32]

Notwithstanding the voter turnout, Dobkin was ecstatic. He had no hall for his victory party; he celebrated at home instead. "The house was full of people," he recalls. "They were dancing and kissing each other. It was like delirium. It really was. It was a real, honest outpouring of emotion.

"It was like a David slaying a Goliath," says Dobkin. "The little guy really beat the big guy. It was so reassuring to know that, once in a while, the little guy can beat the big machine and that people aren't stupid and that the people understand. It re-energizes your faith in the political system."

"I don't think Marty Dobkin got elected, I think my father got defeated," opines Jim Murray. "And that's not a slight against Marty Dobkin. He was in the right place at the right time…. It could have been … open the phone book and write the guy's name down and he would have won the election, in all probability. The mood of the public was that there's too much development, it's going too fast, and we need to stop and have a second look and say 'Slow down'."

In other parts of the Greater Toronto Area, reformers were also finding receptive audiences. In the City of Toronto, almost a year earlier, David Crombie had cruised to victory over old-guard politicians Tony O'Donohue and David Rotenberg (or "Tony Rotenberg" as Crombie liked to call them).

Martin Dobkin and the council-elect, including Streetsville's Hazel McCallion, would have little time to savour their triumphs. The painstaking task of building a city—a people's city—lay before them. Being critics, even constructive critics, would not be enough. They would have to be architects of a new civic culture, amid continuing conflict, internal and external. Nobody predicted that their work would be easy.

Farewell, Town of Streetsville

7

When the *Regional Municipality of Peel Act* was signed into law in June 1973, the battle for Streetsville was over. During the summer that followed, as candidates began jumping into the ring for the elections for the new City of Mississauga, the community started to come to terms with its fate. After December 31, 1973, Streetsville as an incorporated municipality would be no more.

In the battle against amalgamation, the town had proven itself to be a place with spirit. Such a municipality, many believed, needed an occasion, before joining the new city, for its citizens to celebrate their accomplishments. In August, town council decided it was time to begin planning a series of farewell festivities. Reeve Bob Weylie was appointed chairman of the "Special Committee re Town Closing Ceremonies." Council named several other active citizens to help put the events together—including Ralph Hunter, chairman of the parks and recreation board, Gloria Goodings of the planning board, Joan Laurie of the daycare centre board, and Betty Graham of the historical society, among others. Councillor Fred Kingsford joined Reeve Weylie in acting on council's behalf, and Councillor Fred Dineley was appointed to represent the library board.

The resolution establishing the committee gave the chairman authority to name additional members. "It is my intention to appoint representatives from other Boards and Committees as we go along, so that all areas of the Towns [sic] administration will be represented," wrote Weylie in an August 29 letter to the committee. These executive powers were used to bring on several members to help plan for the occasion, including Gary Clipperton of the town's promotional committee and his brother, Jon, who was on the arena board.[1]

STREETSVILLE DAYS

When the committee first met on Wednesday, September 12, members arrived with several proposals: to have a grand launch of the new plan for the town core, to organize a celebrities' hockey game, and to hold a street dance, among other ideas. Within minutes, the brainstorming exercise filled several sheets of chart paper. It was quickly agreed that more than one function should be held, to ensure that there would be something for all ages and tastes. The committee concurred at that first meeting that the celebrations should be named "Streetsville Days" and should commence on Monday, October 29, and continue until Sunday, November 4.

That did not leave much time to prepare. Fortunately, the members worked together effectively. Enthusiastic offers of assistance from the service clubs and the chamber of commerce were quickly forthcoming.

Just after Thanksgiving, with all signs pointing to an excellent week of festivities, Weylie launched the marketing phase.

"Streetsville Days are intended to provide something of interest and delight for all the people of Streetsville," the reeve assured in a press release. "Our Municipal Council has had the support of the vast majority of our people ever since we were elected, and the Council feels it is time to express its appreciation. This feeling is shared by the Service Clubs and Merchants participating in the project."

Continued Weylie: "As we approach the end of Streetsville's days as an independent community after a history of over 100 years, the time is appropriate for a celebration that will continue in the memories of our residents and neighbours. I hope that everyone will take advantage of the opportunity."[2]

Many did. Things kicked off on Monday evening, October 29, with the official opening of the refurbished downtown core. Dignitaries and spectators proceeded from the town hall to the cenotaph in a candlelight parade led by the Lorne Scots Regimental Pipes and Drums. A temporary stage had been erected at the cenotaph. Mayor McCallion officiated, flanked by husband Sam (representing the chamber of commerce) and Reeve Weylie. Premier Bill Davis, perhaps still somewhat uneasy after his very cold reception in Streetsville just a few months earlier, received a more polite greeting on this occasion. Some noticeable improvements had been made to the downtown during the summer—new plant boxes, repairs to sidewalks, and enhancements to many shops. Vic Johnston was hoisted by a public utilities commission truck to pull a string which turned on some new, fancy streetlights. Recently completed plans for future improvements were also unveiled.

Mississauga's mayor-elect, Martin Dobkin, participated in another part of the cenotaph proceedings—the presentation of the Streetsville crest to the new City of Mississauga "for safekeeping."

Tuesday, October 30, was Sports Day. There was free admission to the Streetsville Derbys' hockey game and a figure skating show by Streetsville's very own Canada Games stars, Allan Carson and Linda

Tasker, along with members of the Streetsville Figure Skating Club.

The Derbys lost 5-3 to Burlington. Perhaps more entertaining, therefore, was the broomball game between a squad of town councillors and employees—nicknamed "Hazel's Hurricanes"—and a team made up of Streetsville merchants.

Although she was a very able hockey player (and a long-time promoter of women's hockey), the mayor was not on the town's squad; she was the referee. If the members of the Hazel's Hurricanes team presumed they would enjoy an easy ride because the referee was one of their own, they were mistaken. Not long after the opening face-off, McCallion assigned a penalty to Councillor Graydon Petty—for falling. The Hurricanes never fully recovered from that; the play was in their zone for most of the game.

The merchants put on an outstanding performance. Brothers Gord and Lorne Bentley, as well as Gerry Brennenstuhl, Stanley Campbell, Eric Ladner, Stan Turner, and "Mr. IGA" (Burt Johnston) were in good form for their 1-0 victory.

Wednesday was designated Kids' Day, and the Streetsville Lions were the sponsors. Five local schools organized Hallowe'en parties. Later that afternoon, a costumed street dance began on Queen Street.

Friday was Teen Day, and a dance was organized at the Streetsville Community Hall from 9 p.m. to midnight.

Saturday was perhaps the highlight of the week. At about noon, the entertainment kicked off throughout Streetsville. There was Magician Kazan (Bill Patrick), a Rotary Food Tent in the core area, along with a Legion Pub Tent. Entertainer Kitty Meredith was on hand with honky-tonk pianist Alan Reid. And if you were still not tired, you could attend the open-air Kinsmen dance that night.

Sunday was a quieter day. The local churches had agreed to orient parts of their Sunday services to the civic theme and to reflect on the obligations which citizens have to their neighbours and communities.[3]

THE RECOGNITION DINNER

On November 30, the Town of Streetsville formally extended its appreciation to all those who had served the municipality in various capacities—on council, as part of the town staff, or on committees, boards, and commissions. The official banquet, held at the Vic Johnston Community Centre, was a sight to behold, remembers Gloria Goodings, one of the attendees.[4]

"It was a dynamite thing, just dynamite," confirms Emmaleen Sabourin, Streetsville's treasurer and a key organizer. It was a formal affair, complete with beautiful centrepieces and candles. There were "eight men with white gloves doing nothing but serving wine." There was an official receiving line, including the mayor, her husband, two councillors at a time, and their wives.[5]

Deputy Reeve Jim Graham articulated the sentiments of many Streetsville residents in a prayer which he wrote for the occasion:

A town, its people, their laughter and tears,
Their labour and leisure, their hopes and their fears.

A place to share this gift of living,
To become involved through an act of giving.

In a town, in a meeting, in a friendship, in a care,
Tonight we give thanks for the blessings we share.[6]

Graham had another reason to be proud. The dozens of people who were honoured that evening received a silver plate with the town's crest engraved in the middle. The crest (which was actually close to being a coat of arms) was Graham's baby. A few suggested designs had been put out in 1972, and even published in the local papers, but they never struck a chord. One Friday afternoon in 1973, remembers Graham, the need became pressing. The county wanted a crest for an official publication, but

The Streetsville town crest, designed by Deputy Reeve Jim Graham in consultation with the Streetsville Historical Society's Mary Manning and head librarian Elizabeth Colley, recognizes the significance of founder Timothy Street (with strands of timothy grass), the Credit River, power generation, the salmon fishery, pine and sugar maple trees, religious institutions, grain, and the brick industry.

Streetsville still did not have one. Graham put everything else aside and went to meet with historian Mary Manning, librarian Elizabeth Colley, and others. He wanted to make sure that what emerged reflected the municipality's history, industry, and culture. That weekend, he laboured over the design, which was well received by everyone he asked for an opinion. "The following Friday, these things were stuck on all the town vehicles, and all the small ones were on the town letterhead and everything else."[7] It was also a hit with many local organizations, a few of which sometimes use it to this day.

GETTING READY FOR AMALGAMATION

The task of preparing for the amalgamation brought with it administrative challenges. But because the election of the first Mississauga city council took place on October 1—a full three months before the successful candidates would officially take office—there was time to get ready. The mayor-elect and councillors-elect began meeting as the "Mississauga City Organizational Committee" on October 25, 1973, to deal with critical start-up and transitional issues.

The Minutes of the meeting held on December 28, 1973, indicate that "Mrs. McCallion expressed her disappointment in the [adequacy of the] arrangements." But the number of topics covered and the various agreements reached ensured that the preparations were far more thorough than has been the case with more-recent municipal amalgamations in Ontario. Among the issues discussed and/or resolved:

• It was reported that "adequate facilities for staff are presently available in the Town of Mississauga Municipal offices and neither the Streetsville nor Port Credit Municipal Offices will be required to house any of the municipal administration staff." The *Regional Municipality of Peel Act* had, however, guaranteed jobs to the employees of the former municipalities for at least one year. Municipal staff would continue to use Streetsville's town hall well into 1974 as they made the transition to new quarters.

• It was decided that the Streetsville town hall would be required for police purposes even after the transition period. The new City of Mississauga would lease the building to the Peel Regional Police at $3.50 per square foot.

• The mayor would be paid $20,000 per year, and the councillors would get $10,000.

• The Streetsville Public Library Board was active in drafting key principles for the administration of the amalgamated library system. These included the statement that at least one member from each of the boards of the three existing municipalities should be appointed to the new library board for the city; that remuneration for library employees become standardized; and the somewhat vague principle of "centralization of strategy and resource allocation, balanced by decentralization of operating authority and accountability." At the suggestion of Councillor-elect David Culham (Ward 6), a statement was added supporting the need to co-ordinate services, wherever possible, with those of the Peel Board of Education. These points were approved in principle by the inter-library co-ordinating committee and would be presented to the new library board. Streetsville's librarian, Elizabeth Colley, recalls that her salary nearly doubled shortly after amalgamation.[8]

Mississauga's Lou Parsons, who had served on town council since 1967, was appointed regional chairman on July 31, despite the complaints of the provincial opposition politicians. Premier Davis personally made the selection.[9] Parsons, 39, had written to Davis on January 29, 1973, less than a week after the Mohawk College presentation, to express interest in the position.[10] Several weeks later, he gave up his duties as a partner in Parsons-Taylor Realty, one of the largest real-estate firms in the county.[11] His regional appointment was controversial in Peel. Predictably, Mississauga Mayor Chic Murray was ecstatic. Hazel McCallion's response was an abrupt "no comment."[12]

There may have been some hesitation within the cabinet about appointing Parsons. John Kruger, the executive assistant to the chairman of Metropolitan Toronto, wrote to Davis on July 6, 1973, expressing his interest in the position. He stated that he had met with Minister John White and that he understood there to be "a possibility of my being considered as a 'compromise' candidate" for the Peel chairmanship.[13]

Kruger's appointment would have been unlikely even if Parsons had been passed over. The new regional chairmen for Halton, Durham, and Hamilton-Wentworth, whose appointments were announced at the same time as Peel's, were all residents of their respective regions. Kruger's letter conceded that his knowledge of Peel was not extensive. Moreover, appointing an official from the Metro chairman's office would have been bad optics, casting Metro as the dominant neighbour.

At one point, White generated a handwritten list of possible candidates for the regional chairman's post. It is not clear how much consideration (if any) was being given to each of these individuals. Some of the names might have ended up on the list because of informal recommendations or because of direct expressions of interest. At any rate, there are eight names on the list. Parsons is listed first, followed by Warden Ivor McMullin. The third name on the list is Hazel McCallion's. Scribbled alongside her name are the words "No—Kennedy," which appears to be an indication that objections had been expressed by Peel South MPP Doug Kennedy.[14]

Parsons moved quickly after October 1 to get Mississauga's mayor-elect and councillors-elect engaged in regional business. The mayor and all nine councillors would automatically assume seats on the regional council. Their first official meeting was held on October 19, 1973, more than two months before the inauguration of the amalgamated lower-tier municipalities. John White, who assisted Lieutenant Governor Ross Macdonald in presiding over the occasion, was especially enthusiastic in his praise of the councillor-elect for the Streetsville Ward. Indeed, his outgoing correspondence files for the second half of 1973 contain only one letter of congratulations following the local elections in Peel. That letter was to Hazel McCallion.[15]

Streetsville Treasurer Emmaleen Sabourin assumed a leadership role in helping her town's staff to smoothly effect the transition. She recalls being dismayed at the state of Mississauga's financial management. One of her tasks was to set up a formal accounts payable unit—something which the Town of Mississauga lacked. Ensuring that all employees did not see a diminution in their benefits was also a challenge, Sabourin says. Streetsville's employees had Ontario Health Insurance coverage for their spouses, but in the Town of Mississauga this benefit was only extended to the wives of male employees. There was some resistance at first to incorporating the non-discriminatory Streetsville scheme into the package for the new City of Mississauga; Sabourin remembers having to speak out at council to get it corrected.[16]

A special steering committee had already been established to co-ordinate the start-up of the Peel Regional Police. The committee, which was chaired by Judge Barry Shapiro, included Streetsville Councillor Doug Spencer. Plans were made to standardize salaries and benefits to the highest levels then existing. The salaries for the Streetsville rank-and-file officers were, for the most part, already slightly higher than in the other jurisdictions. A common telephone number (453-3311) would be set up, new insignia and a common colour adopted, renovations undertaken, and initial plans drawn up for new police headquarters. The Peel force would not serve the new Town of Caledon, which would continue to be looked after by the Ontario Provincial Police.

One of the members of the new police commission, appointed in November 1973, was from Streetsville—former reeve Bill Appleton got the provincial nod. He had supported police amalgamation as a member of the 1971-72 Regional Police Force Study Committee.[17]

As early as February 1972, Darcy McKeough (the provincial treasurer at the time) had concluded that creating regional police forces was an expensive proposition. In a letter to cabinet colleague John Yaremko, McKeough noted that the cost increases could be attributed to "uniform bargaining agreements (usually based on the highest in the areas before amalgamating the forces), increased transportation costs, a greater number of management and administrative personnel, accommodation requirements, and improved communication systems."[18]

The Streetsville Public Utilities Commission actually survived amalgamation. The region assumed responsibility for water, although the PUC continued to look after electricity. By late 1975, however, the commission had paid off its debentures, and amalgamation with Hydro Mississauga was once again being actively discussed. Just over a year later, the PUC was finally relegated to history. Streetsville's Ron Walker became vice chairman of Hydro Mississauga.

Streetsville's politicians and staff worked hard to efficiently wrap up the business of the town. The municipality finished the year with a surplus of $85,000. Although members of council agreed to allow the surplus to go forward to the new city, Jim

Graham recalls that there were some second thoughts. "The only thing I had misgivings about ... is that we could have put the funds into a community hall or swimming pool," he says.[19]

Part of the surplus can be attributed to a rather unusual grant from the provincial government. On August 14, 1973, Mayor McCallion wrote to Minister John White, asking the province to reimburse Streetsville for the cost of the 1968 *Boundary Study* ($18,376) and for the consultants retained by Streetsville in 1973 to help the town draft its alternative proposals ($12,761), for a total of $31,137. Argued McCallion: "As the Town of Streetsville will be ceasing to exist as a Municipality as of December 31st of this year, we have been faced with additional costs which were not anticipated at the time that we established the budget for 1973."

Provincial staff in the Local Government Organization Branch were strenuously opposed to this request. In a letter to assistant deputy minister Peter Honey, branch director Ron Farrow argued:

> To make this grant to Streetsville would open the whole question of looking back over the records and paying the municipalities of Niagara, the municipalities in Hamilton and Wentworth, the municipalities East of Metro, in Waterloo, in Sudbury, the great sums of money that they brought to the preparation of their own views and their own aspirations to place before ... the Government of Ontario.

In the margins of one of the memoranda distributed internally on this issue, an unidentified civil servant wrote sarcastically: "Streetsville reverses itself—can't afford these studies, how on earth could [it] be the basis of a separate munic.??"

John White overruled the staff and approved the grant.[20]

THE FINAL TOWN COUNCIL MEETING

Lou Parsons announced that the new region would not be launched with any New Year's fanfare because "[p]eople are simply too busy

New Year's Eve to take time off for something as minor as the start of a new region." He added that when the Township of Toronto became the Town of Mississauga on January 1, 1968, the only people who showed up to usher out the old municipality and welcome the new one were councillors, department heads, and those staff members who had to be there.[21]

In Streetsville, it was a different story. Many residents put their parties on hold to bid farewell to their town. There was not even standing room in the modest council chamber as the town council held its final meeting. It took place at almost the last possible moment—7 p.m. on New Year's Eve.

"There were a lot of glum faces that night," Frank Dowling, Streetsville's first mayor, told me in 1997.[22] All councillors had a chance to speak, and they lamented the municipality's demise, while urging their fellow residents to work hard to make the new city a success. Former long-time local politician Bill Arch was on hand to officially present to council the 1858 charter incorporating the Village of Streetsville. As the evening drew to a close, Mayor McCallion took off her chain of office and handed it to Al Betts, president of the chamber of commerce. (The chamber had donated the first mayoral chain in 1962.) Betts, in turn, presented it to Gianna Williams, president of the Streetsville Historical Society, for display and safekeeping.

As a municipality, Streetsville had seen Confederation, the introduction of the automobile, both world wars, the baby boom, Trudeaumania, and the growing prominence of multiculturalism. But it would greet the next millennium as part of a much bigger municipality—one that would rapidly become one of Canada's largest cities.

As they filed out of the town hall on that cold, brisk night, the people of Streetsville wondered what would happen to their community. When the clock struck midnight and champagne bottles were opened, it must have felt like the end of an era.

Afterword:
A Community
in Transition

New Year's Day, 1974, was much like any other in Streetsville. The community was quiet, except for a few church services and the comings and goings of those who were spending the day with family and friends.

Streetsville's loss of town status was not immediately apparent. The local constables were now part of the Peel Regional Police, but they stood on call much as they always had. Even the volunteer fire department, officially dissolved, knew that it might yet be called into service.

On Wednesday, January 2, the employees of the former Town of Streetsville still went to work, much as usual—and, in most cases, to similar jobs. Outside the town hall, the sign still said "Town of Streetsville Municipal Offices." The Streetsville bylaws remained in force.

But changes were soon apparent. Anyone calling the town hall on January 2 would, as usual, be greeted by a friendly, helpful voice. This time, however, the salutation was, "Good afternoon [pause] … City of Mississauga."[1] Streetsville's former reeve, deputy reeve, and councillors did not have any more municipal meetings penciled into their agenda books.

Hazel McCallion, of course, had a full agenda. As the councillor representing the new city's Streetsville Ward, she asserted that the only hope for the long-term viability of the amalgamated municipality lay in its potential to maintain within its borders a number of genuine, distinct neighbourhoods.

On January 8, Mississauga city council held its inaugural meeting at Glenforest Secondary School. This was still 13 years before the completion of a state-of-the-art civic centre with an impressive council chamber large enough to accommodate 350 people—the existing city hall would simply not have been adequate for the anticipated audience.

Dobkin's mayoralty was a shaky one. The political novice soon found himself recoiling after a few gaffes. He seemed well-intentioned, however, and with his elected colleagues he endeavoured to introduce reforms. Consultants' reports were commissioned in an effort to bring in a coherent, long-term vision for the city and to effect badly needed changes to the municipal bureaucracy. A comprehensive official plan review was undertaken and some long-term priorities were established.[2] But there were sharp divisions on council between the reformers and the old guard. There was sustained and highly publicized conflict between the (not-always-cohesive) reformist majority on council and the developers. Most of the senior managers who had previously worked for the Town of Mississauga soon decided to pursue their careers elsewhere.

In 1975, on the advice of the city solicitor, Dobkin put forward a resolution, which was passed unanimously (but later criticized by some members of council), to convene a judicial inquiry to investigate never-fully disclosed allegations of illegal conduct in some parts of the administration of the former Town of Mississauga. Chic Murray, the last mayor of the Town of Mississauga, charged that the whole exercise was a politically motivated fishing expedition. Regional chairman (and former Town of Mississauga politician) Lou Parsons claimed to have proof of that when he stood up at regional council and revealed that Dobkin's executive assistant, who quietly resigned shortly before the inquiry was called, had sworn an affidavit asserting that the mayor's motives were political. Dobkin angrily denied this accusation. The inquiry was eventually shut down by the courts on the grounds that the city was exceeding its authority by probing the former town as well as the existing or former special-purpose bodies. Defamation lawsuits against Dobkin and McCallion, among others, were also eventually thrown out of court.[3]

Dobkin ran for re-election in 1976, but lost to Councillor Ron Searle. Searle's was also a one-term mayoralty. The next election, in 1978, saw him defeated by Streetsville's Hazel McCallion—prompting some commentators to remark that Mississauga had not taken over Streetsville but that Streetsville had taken over Mississauga.

McCallion has presided over continued rapid growth in Mississauga. Indeed, most of the city's residents—who today number more than 625,000 and come from all parts of the world—have known no other Mississauga mayor. She was there in 1979 when most of the city was evacuated because of a chemical hazard resulting from a major train derailment. (It was called the "Mississauga Miracle" because there were no casualties.) She was there when the Duke and Duchess of York opened the architecturally controversial new civic centre (still in the vicinity of the former McLaughlin structure) in 1987 and when her dream of a Living Arts Centre was realized in 1997. She has been in the thick of countless battles with the region, the province, and Ottawa over property taxes, downloading of costs, airport noise, highways, waste disposal, and public transit financing, among other matters. On February 14, 2001, hundreds of well-wishers turned out for a reception marking the 80th birthday of a mayor who remains full of energy.

McCallion has prided herself on a pay-as-you-go fiscal philosophy and on council's decision to freeze or reduce taxes for most of the 1990s. However, with the era of major "greenfields" developments now nearly at an end, tax increases can be expected—despite the city's reserves. Mississauga's infrastructure will need expensive upgrades or replacement within a compressed time frame, rather than over a period of many years as is the case in cities which developed more gradually. Moreover, the relatively low population densities in much of the city will prompt some difficult choices for residents and their elected officials—accept urban intensification and in-fill development or face the escalating per capita costs required to sustain the municipality's infrastructure and transportation system. And without a high-quality transit system, the traffic congestion will only get worse. McCallion has been recently raising these concerns frequently. She has likewise been calling for strengthened Greater Toronto Area co-ordinating institutions/mechanisms to deal with the common challenges facing the municipalities within Toronto's orbit.

What happened to the reform/neighbourhood movement which helped define the amalgamation debates and the Mississauga election campaign of 1973? Although there is no single, clear response, the following possibilities should be considered:

• Some of the reformers' objectives were incorporated into the day-to-day business of the municipality. There are, for example, more opportunities for public input. Generally speaking, developers face tougher restrictions and obligations.

• After the mid-1970s, economic growth has been slower than it was for much of the post-World War II period. The middle class' concern with quality-of-life issues and its willingness to embrace progressive politics seem to emerge following periods of extended prosperity rather than economic uncertainty or stagnation. Although Mississauga was always in the path of significant development, the broader (and more ambivalent) economic indicators may have contributed to shifting the political focus to one which was more receptive to that growth as well as to government retrenchment.

• The reformers on the 1974-76 council not only encountered tremendous resistance from the developers and from those local, regional, and provincial politicians who did not embrace the reform ethos, but they were not able to forge a cohesive and enduring community coalition on which they could consistently rely for support and a measure of stability while navigating the stormy waters.* The city's residents' associations and

---

* Despite the general desire for change which was apparent in the results of the 1973 election, as well as the widespread public concerns about the *ancien régime,* sustaining the reform impulses and channelling them to support specific policy initiatives were no easy matters. Machiavelli perhaps made a valid observation when he wrote that "it should be considered that nothing is more difficult to handle, more doubtful of success, nor more dangerous to manage than to put oneself at the head of introducing new orders. For the introducer has all those who benefit from the old orders as enemies, and he has lukewarm defenders in all those who might benefit from the new orders. This lukewarmness arises partly from fear of adversaries who have the laws on their side and partly from the incredulity of men, who do not truly believe in new things unless they come to have a firm experience of them." (*The Prince*, H. Mansfield translation, Chicago: University of Chicago Press, 1985, pp. 23-24.) The institutional framework within which decisions are made is also an important variable. On a non-partisan council, individual members are arguably more vulnerable to the pressure (or electoral threats) exerted by assertive, well-heeled lobbyists or vested interests who have a lot to lose if a proposal is adopted than what would be the case if the council members' fate was closely linked to that of a disciplined political party, as it is in most parliaments operating under the Westminster system. In other words, a strong team is harder to thwart than a loose alliance of individual political entrepreneurs who rely more on themselves than each other for re-election.

neighbourhood groups, although concerned about the policies and direction of the old council and generally supportive (at least initially) of the Dobkin council, were fragmented and had few resources. They often focussed almost exclusively on immediate issues or threats rather than helping to implement an overall, long-term vision for the municipality. The Streetsville Ward's high levels of civic engagement and political awareness were arguably not reflected in much of the rest of the city.

There have been recent indications, however, of a renaissance of reform/neighbourhood principles.[4] There is more talk about conservation, more criticism of often-monolithic, impersonal suburban communities, concern about the paramountcy of the automobile, and more discussion about better public transportation, not to mention social concerns such as poverty, homelessness, and the serious shortage of affordable housing. Neo-conservative politicians who tout tax cuts, less government, and the free market as solutions to every problem are now finding their audiences to be less receptive than they were just a few years ago.

OTHER POST-AMALGAMATION EVENTS

Hazel McCallion and Jack Graham met again—in court. In July 1982, Judge Ernest West found that McCallion clearly violated the *Municipal Conflict of Interest Act* on November 2, 1981, when she discussed and voted on a resolution to release for secondary planning/development study a large tract of land that included her family's five-acre property. West ruled that this was a "substantial" but "*bona fide* error in judgement" and that the mayor could remain in office. Graham was the citizen who brought the complaint forward.[5]

Bill Davis did not have to worry about the Streetsville electorate in future races for his riding; redistribution took place before the 1975 provincial election. An exciting contest ensued in the new Mississauga North constituency, which included Streetsville. The

Conservative candidate, Terry Jones, edged out New Democrat David Busby, 11,001 votes to 10,616. Busby, a minister who had served at Streetsville's Trinity Anglican Church, came out ahead in the majority of the Streetsville polls—a first for the NDP. Busby was widely respected for his work with the poor and marginalized. His extensive résumé included his role in helping to establish Street Haven, a Toronto inner-city shelter.

Jones, also a Streetsville resident, had previously worked on Davis's campaigns. However, in a letter dated March 17, 1972, he warned the premier that many people who had supported the government "are disturbed ... that future regionalism for the Peel area may ignore this desire [in Streetsville] to preserve a viable community feeling."[6] Province-wide, the Tories emerged from the 1975 election with a much poorer showing than their commanding 1971 victory, and they were left with a minority government.*

Doug Kennedy, then the Conservative MPP for Mississauga South, does not doubt that there was political fallout from the creation of regional governments. "We went too far, too fast," he concedes. "That cost us."[7]

Many of the key local figures in Streetsville in 1973 went on to do very well—an indication of the strength of the former town's administrative team. Len McGillivary became deputy clerk of the City of Mississauga and on at least one occasion turned down the clerk's position. Gord Bentley, Streetsville's deputy fire chief, was Mississauga's fire chief from 1978 to 1992. He also served a term as president of the Canadian Association of Fire Chiefs. John Wiersma, the PUC manager, went to Wasaga Beach Hydro to organize a major expansion, later became manager of Pickering Hydro, and now

---

* In 1975, the Progressive Conservatives won 51 out of 125 seats. The NDP took 38 and the Liberals 35. The 1971 results (for an assembly of 117 seats) were 78, 19, and 20, respectively.

heads Veridian Connections, an amalgamated corporation (which includes Pickering) created as a result of the recent hydro restructuring. Don Fletcher, Streetsville's police chief, had a successful career as a senior member of the Peel Regional Police. Streetsville's treasurer, Emmaleen Sabourin, went back to the private sector in 1976, but later joined the Mississauga Library System where she oversaw the finances, before becoming the mayor's executive assistant. Ward Allen, the Toronto lawyer who served part-time as Streetsville's solicitor, was made a judge just before amalgamation. In the early 1980s, he led the highly publicized judicial inquiry into the care of Kim Anne Popen by the Sarnia-Lambton Children's Aid Society. Peter Mah, one of the student leaders of the Core '73 project, is now a senior public servant for the Government of Manitoba.

The ranks of the old Streetsville team are thinning. Reeve Robert Weylie, Vic Johnston, Sam McCallion, parade marshal extraordinaire Frank Haddon, public works manager Keith Cowan, deputy police chief Ted Rutledge, historian Mary Manning, SCORE chairman Blake Goodings, and library board chairman Ian Ferguson are among those who have passed on. A number of the firefighters and other prominent local volunteers have also died, as have some of the key players from the Town of Mississauga and the Province of Ontario, including Chic Murray and John White.

CHANGES IN STREETSVILLE

Streetsville has seen many changes since amalgamation. In 1974, it was still surrounded by vast tracts of sparsely populated land. Highways 403 and 407 had not yet been constructed. Except for Streetsville, Malton, and the fledgling Meadowvale development, there was no built-up area in Mississauga north of Burnhamthorpe Road. In fact, if you were driving along Burnhamthorpe you would not be able to cross the Credit River—the bridge had yet to be constructed.

As predicted even before the 1968 *Boundary Study*, residential and industrial areas now completely surround Streetsville. But throughout the 1970s and early 1980s, the prospect still presented problems to many in Streetsville, including the business community. In the years immediately following 1973, not a great deal was done to bring to fruition the long-term objectives identified by the Core '73 team. The downtown still lacked visual appeal, as if its heyday had passed.

In 1987, a new *Streetsville District Plan* was approved. In the years that followed, a great deal more work has been undertaken, so that the core now looks better than ever. It is bright, clean, with quaint alleys and well-restored historic buildings. It has old-fashioned lamp posts with regularly changing banners to mark the seasons or to promote community celebrations. Sidewalk improvements have been stepped up, and a "Millennium Clock" was unveiled beside the cenotaph. The area immediately around the cenotaph looks more than ever like a real town square. Many recommendations from Core '73 and subsequent reports have at last been implemented. The Streetsville Business Improvement Association has a reputation for effectiveness and persistence.

Aesthetic improvements aside, a sense of community endures in Streetsville. Most local businesses and many residents still list their addresses as "Streetsville, Ontario." Many meetings on local issues are well attended. The Bread and Honey Festival draws tens of thousands of visitors but still feels like a small-town Homecoming. Streetsville has its own jazz festival, Canada Day festivities, and Santa Claus parade. The historical society lives on, as do many of the service clubs and other local organizations—although in some cases with diminished memberships. The Vic Johnston Community Centre remains under the direction of a separate board, and the more-recently developed David J. Culham Trail has fostered an appreciation for the community's natural amenities. Consolidationists could

Prime Minister Pierre Trudeau inspects a hot-air balloon at the second Streetsville Bread and Honey Festival. It took place on June 1, 1974, less than half a year after amalgamation. The festival continues to be held annually on the first weekend in June. It is one of Mississauga's most successful events. *Photograph courtesy of Paul McCallion (family album).*

plausibly contend that these examples substantiate their thesis that the absence of municipal status does not affect a community's ability to maintain its identity. On the other hand, critics could validly reply that the two parts of Mississauga which have most effectively preserved their distinctiveness (Streetsville and Port Credit) are the two places that were once incorporated entities with their own local governments. Other communities, such as Cooksville, Dixie, Lakeview, and Erindale, are barely distinguishable from the rest of the city—fewer and fewer people identify with those villages.

Although Streetsville's wishes were rejected in 1973, its efforts were probably not in vain. Never had the community been so united and so mobilized. The events of that year arguably encouraged residents to cherish their town's social assets more than ever and to renew their interest in civic engagement. This has, no doubt, helped

Streetsville to hold on to its community spirit. And if we believe some of the compelling recent literature on "social capital,"* residents' quality of life and general contentment may depend, at least in part, on an ethos that counters the individualism, materialism, and anomie which threaten to overrun our society.

Between the mid-1970s and early 1990s, there were few amalgamations in Ontario; the regional government schemes of the late 1960s and early 1970s had left a bitter taste in many parts of the province. But in 1996, the province launched a dramatic push to consolidate municipalities. During the past few years, the number of municipalities has been reduced by approximately 350, with almost 1,800 fewer municipal politicians. Despite the 1998 formation of a single, one-tier government for the area formerly covered by the Municipality of Metropolitan Toronto, no changes have been announced for Peel Region or the three other "905" regions in the Greater Toronto Area—Halton, York, and Durham. In early 2001, the government finally let it be known that it would relent in its aggressive pursuit of municipal mergers.

The recent arguments for amalgamation have been somewhat different from those advanced by the Robarts and Davis administrations. Rarely does one now hear about equity or more effective planning. Instead, political hot buttons are pushed simplistically

---

* One of the most impressive books of recent years is Robert D. Putnam's *Bowling Alone—The Collapse and Revival of American Community* (New York: Simon & Schuster, 2000). In this detailed study, Putnam examines the extent, causes, and the likely adverse consequences of the decline in civic engagement in the United States. In an earlier book, *Making Democracy Work* (Princeton University Press, 1993), Putnam studies the Italian regional governments, which were created in 1970. The contrast between the effective regional administrations and those with very poor results is striking. Putnam endeavours to demonstrate that the level of civic engagement is an important variable in explaining the relative success or failure of these governments.

and cynically. Reducing the number of politicians is somehow equated with increasing accountability. Bigger municipal units are sold as automatic guarantees that taxes will be lower, with little, if any, credible evidence.[8]

Indeed, Peel's regional government was not even a year old before the province was quietly expressing concerns about the rapidly escalating spending and taxes, despite the provincial mitigation grants and despite the fact that cost savings were not seriously anticipated by Queen's Park in the first place. On September 4, 1974, Treasurer John White wrote to Regional Chairman Lou Parsons:

> Excessive spending, regardless of which level of government raises the tax revenues to pay for it, is less than reasonable at this time. I am reluctant to interfere in the internal affairs of the Region or the area municipalities, but I feel compelled to ask that you critically review your spending priorities with a view to minimizing the overall impact on regional taxpayers.
>
> I suggest that every endeavour be made to contain the overall increase in property tax levels to 10% above comparable 1973 levels. The Province is making substantially enriched transfer payments available in the region and this must now be complemented by fiscal restraint at the regional and area levels.[9]

The 10-percent target was not met. The average ratepayer in the new city saw an increase of 16.88 percent in 1974.[10]

LOOKING TO THE FUTURE

Will Streetsville preserve its identity? Will the strong community spirit live on, or will it die with the long-time residents? Only time will tell, of course, but there will be many challenges, as even Hazel McCallion acknowledges.[11] The explosion of big-box retail, the challenge of recruiting community volunteers, and a rather apathetic disposition to civic and local affairs demonstrated by many people (not only in Mississauga) who move into a new community simply to hide behind wooden fences are reasons for concern. Without municipal status and a council interested specifically in its affairs, Streetsville's task is probably all the more formidable. Since 1978, Streetsville has not even had its own ward on Mississauga city council. Two decades have now passed since the *Streetsville Review* folded, after more than 130 years in business.*

We will eventually have the answer. The people of what was once the Town of Streetsville and its surrounding area will ultimately decide whether the community becomes a historical footnote or whether it will be a dynamic, thriving place, a good place to grow up, where neighbours help neighbours. Those who are too occupied trying to make a dollar, those who believe that only short-term economic goals are important, might not fret either way. But there will be a few people, I am sure, who would regret the passing of a community—its warts and all—and who would reflect fondly on the Streetsville that was and the Streetsville that could have been.

---

* The *Streetsville Booster* became the *Mississauga Booster* in the early 1980s as its distribution area gradually expanded to cover all of northwest Mississauga. In 1998, the paper went citywide. In early 2001, however, it was purchased by Metroland Printing, Publishing and Distribution, and became the *Streetsville/Meadowvale Booster*, with separate Streetsville and Meadowvale editions on alternating weeks.

The Millennium Clock was unveiled at Streetsville's year 2000 Canada Day festivities. It is located near the corner of Queen and Main Streets, in the heart of downtown Streetsville. *Photograph by Stephen Uhraney for the* Booster. *Reprinted with permission.*

Appendix

The Final Council Meeting
*of the Corporation of the Town of Streetsville**
Monday, December 31, 1973
7 p.m.
Streetsville Town Hall

Mayor Hazel McCallion: I would like to call to order the final meeting of the Corporation of the Town of Streetsville for Monday, December the 31st—a town founded in 1820 by Timothy Street, incorporated in 1858.

I have a motion for the adoption of the Minutes of the regular meeting of December the 28th, 1973. Moved by Reeve Weylie, seconded by Councillor Spencer: "That the Minutes of the special meeting of council held on December 27th, 1973, be adopted as transcribed and circulated."

Any discussion on the motion? All in favour? Any opposed? Carried unanimously, Mr. Clerk.

I'd like to welcome tonight members of the Town of Streetsville who have come to attend the final meeting of this great town. I hope that later on, some of you, if you so wish, will have the opportunity to make statements or to ask any questions, and we hope that you will participate at a later time in the meeting.

---

* The author thanks Bob Keeping for his permission to prepare and publish this transcript of his audio recording of the meeting.

Tonight, we hope that most of the business of the past year has been completed. We held a meeting this afternoon at four o'clock, and I think we attended to all the business, except one item that I would now like to place before council.

As you know, we are very proud of our downtown core program, which we had the pleasure and privilege of implementing. We feel that what we have done in 1973 to the downtown core of Streetsville will remain as a symbol, as well as an example, of how we felt about this great town; that it should be rehabilitated so that it will last for many years to come as a centre of this great area. I have a motion by Councillor Watkins, seconded by Councillor Spencer: "That the report of Core '73, entitled *A Downtown Rehabilitation Program,* be adopted by this council and that the report be forwarded to the City of Mississauga for consideration and implementation of Phase II."

Any discussion on the motion? All in favour? Any opposed? Carried.

A former reeve of this municipality, Reeve William Arch, tonight has brought to this meeting the Charter of the Town of Streetsville. It was assented to the 24th of July, 1858. It's a very interesting document, and I will not read it this evening, members of council, but I would hope that we could obtain copies of this, as I feel that all members of the present council would like a copy to keep. And so I have asked the reeve if we could reproduce these and distribute a copy to all of you. It's a very interesting document, and I would just like to read the concluding statement: "The said Village of Streetsville shall be entitled to receive, from the said Township of Toronto, such share of all money apportioned to such Township from the Upper Canada Municipalities Fund prior to the passing of this Act, and now unappropriated, as shall bear the same proportion of the whole sum so apportioned to the said Township as the number of ratepayers resident within the said Village as shown by the Collector's Role of the year 1857 bears to the whole number of ratepayers of the said Township."

This is the charter which was granted to the Town of Streetsville in 1858. So we will reproduce this and pass it on to all members of the present council, and in fact, if any members of the audience would like a copy, I'm sure that we would be only too happy to reproduce it. I believe our treasurer feels there is still a few funds in the account to look after that.

The next item on our agenda is a statement on our staff that I would like to make tonight. The staff of the Town of Streetsville has been well looked after in the new City of Mississauga. They received a letter today, welcoming them to the new city and advising them that they are to report to a certain department on January 2, on Wednesday. They have all been located and, as far as I know at this point, happy with the arrangement that has been made for them. I think that … I *know* that members of the council would like to know that this is so—that they have been well looked after in the new City of Mississauga.

In regard to the financial position of the municipality, I am very pleased to report that we will be ending the year without a deficit and that we will be transferring somewhere close to $85,000 surplus to the new City of Mississauga. And I think that this is a tribute to your council, with all the effort that they have put in in the last year and the many projects they have undertaken. And this has been done with the co-operation of the Streetsville Public Utilities Commission. I know our chairman is in the audience tonight, and I would like to say to him how much we appreciate the co-operation of the PUC. We worked very hard this year to conclude all the projects that we hope have made the people of Streetsville happy.

I have a motion—that I don't know who would like the privilege of signing—but this is a motion: "That this council does hereby authorize the transfer to the Archives of Ontario of the records of the municipality as listed in the attachment to the letter dated December 17, 1973, from Mr. D.F. McOuat of the Ontario Archives." These are the Minutes of the council meetings of 1858, correspondence, tax rolls, assessment rolls. There isn't a continuity of these records. The archives have asked for these. They are being turned over to the archives. A microfilmed copy will be made free of charge, and we, in turn, will present that to the Streetsville Historical Society. We hope that the library, early in '74, will have the type of equipment that this microfilm will be able to be shown to the schoolchildren and to the residents of Streetsville, when required or requested.

Is there any member of the audience that would like to speak at this time, as we sign some of these resolutions, and then we will put … How about the first mayor of the Town of Streetsville, Mr. Frank Dowling? Would you like to say a word?

Mr. Frank Dowling: I'm lost for words ... I'm very pleased to be here tonight. I'm glad I read tonight's paper, or otherwise I would have missed it. I feel very humbled that I was given the opportunity of being the first mayor. I'm sorry to say, Madam Mayor, that you are the last mayor of Streetsville. I was hoping that for many years to come ... The predictions that they gave us the night that we were first incorporated as a town weren't too encouraging. One paper quoted five years; I'm glad that we doubled that. So again, I'd like to thank everyone. I know that this council this year has done an excellent job, and I congratulate you on the fight that you have put up and everything else. Again, thank you very much.

Mayor Hazel McCallion: I'd now like to call on a former reeve of the town that's in our audience, Mr. Bill Arch, who was so kind tonight to bring the original charter of the town. Mr. Arch, would you like to come forward and say a few words?

Mr. W.C. Arch: Madam Mayor, councillors: It's quite strange for me to be in here. I haven't been here for quite some time. I am here tonight to make my presence seen at the last council meeting of the Town of Streetsville. I had a great deal to do in the administration in past years, having served on pretty well all bodies of council, including five years as reeve [and] warden of Peel County in 1956. I have worked for several years with our present mayor, on very good terms I might say. And we have done, with the help of council, I think a very good job, and our present council, in finally closing the Town of Streetsville, as I understand, having heard the records, on a very good scale. I wish everybody in Streetsville, the mayor, and the present council the very best in the coming year, and especially to our mayor in her new job on the city council of Mississauga. Thank you.

Mayor Hazel McCallion: Any other members of the audience that would like to make a statement?

If not, we'll go on with the resolution. Moved by Councillor Graydon Petty, seconded by Councillor Jim Watkins: "That this council does hereby authorize the transfer to the Archives of Ontario the records of the

Municipality of Streetsville, as listed in the attached letter dated December 17th, 1973, from Mr. McOuat of the Ontario Archives."

Any discussion on the motion? All in favour? Any opposed? Carried.

I have a motion by Councillor Spencer, seconded by Councillor Rea: "That the pictures, maps, and artifacts listed on Schedule A to this resolution be transferred to the Streetsville Historical Society."

The aerial views of Streetsville presented by Mr. Hope—and I'll just give a short run-down of the things—the picture of the municipal councils of '71/'72 and … 1939 picture, the plaque of the Lions Club Citizen of the Year, the framed picture of the Streetsville Police Department, the unframed picture of the town council, 1962—I don't know where that came from. And the pictures that are on this wall, which are the pictures that the Streetsville Historical Society has assembled of the reeves and the mayors of the Town of Streetsville since its incorporation.

Any discussion on the motion?

Deputy Reeve J.S. Graham: Madam Mayor … if the seals of the Town of Streetsville, the Village of Streetsville, and of the Streetsville Secondary School are on that list?

Mayor Hazel McCallion: Yes—seal of Streetsville Public School, seal of the Village of Streetsville, and seal of the Town of Streetsville.

Deputy Reeve J.S. Graham: Alright. And the chain of office has been deleted from that?

Mayor Hazel McCallion: Yes.

Deputy Reeve J.S. Graham: Thank you.

Mayor Hazel McCallion: Any discussion on the motion?

All in favour? Any opposed? Carried.

At this point, I would like to present to the members of council, if they would come forward starting with Councillor Dineley, a very attractive coloured picture of the 1973 council.

Councillor F.J. Dineley: Thanks, Mayor Hazel.

Mayor Hazel McCallion: You're welcome.

Councillor Rea? The names will be … [The remaining councillors, deputy reeve, and reeve receive the portrait and each, in turn, plants a kiss on the mayor's cheek.]

My husband is here; he noticed!

A Member of Council: He's taking pictures all the time!

Mayor Hazel McCallion: Now is the time that I'm going to call on this council that I can assure you that I'm very proud of, that has been outstanding. In my opinion [the members of council] have been outstanding in the years that I have served as mayor of this municipality and who have supported me, and I can only assure you [they] have only had the interests of the people of Streetsville at heart.

I would now like to call on Councillor King— Fred Kingsford.

Councillor F. Kingsford: Thank you, Madam Mayor. In a few hours, at the stroke of twelve, we begin a new year. This is a beginning and it also is an end, for at this time Streetsville officially disappears from the map. When I consider the strong community spirit which is so much a part of every Streetsvillite, I can't help but feel that, for the overwhelming majority of us, the coming of 1974 will be greeted with mixed feelings.

Today we live in a world where more and more people are questioning our value system. There is a strong need by many to take a close look at some of the values which we have tossed aside in the name of progress. People are in search of a personal identification and, in ever-increasing numbers, they are looking towards the community and the neighbourhood for answers for the ongoing search. Only a few years ago it would have been unheard-of for residents of a community to stop a highway expressway from coming through their neighbourhood or prevent their municipal government from forsaking an older area of a community to a developer.

Together, we fought for what we thought was right. We fought hard, and all should be proud that we did the best we could to preserve what was important to us. Despite our battle, we lost. And when we did, a little of each of us died. Now that the battle is over, it is time to accept the change and co-operate with the new government. In the long run, we, the residents of Streetsville, may discover that being part of the City of Mississauga will provide us with benefits which were unavailable while we were still a small community. As we have in the past, each of us should continue to actively participate in municipal government, ensuring the City of Mississauga, and in particular our community, will continue to thrive.

For more than 100 years, there have been Streetsvillites, and, as members of this community with its particular lifestyle, we have certain qualities and values. The City of Mississauga is gaining a lot more than land and people. It is gaining the qualities and values that we have nurtured over many generations. These are welcomed and needed by any growing community.

Before I leave this council chamber for the last time, I would like to thank the citizens of the Town of Streetsville for the honour and privilege of serving them as a member of this council for the past two years. I thank our mayor, Hazel McCallion, and all fellow council members for their encouragement, support, and understanding during my term of office. These are dedicated people and have served the town well. I shall sorely miss the very close association we had, although we didn't always agree on matters of town business. To the staff of the Town of Streetsville, I say thank you for a job well done. Your co-operation with us has been first class, and I wish each and every one of you success in your new positions in the new City of Mississauga or the Region of Peel. To the boards and commissions of the Town of Streetsville, who have given many hours of their personal time and talents, without remuneration, for the benefit of the citizens of our town, my thanks also. Last but not least, to the police and fire departments, thank you for your protection. I'm sure you will continue to serve the public just as well under the new jurisdiction as you did under the old.

So at midnight, Streetsville fades into history. However, our spirits and beliefs will never die. In time they may. But during the years it will take for this to happen, we will have a lot to offer our municipality and its government. Thank you very much, Madam Mayor.

Mayor Hazel McCallion: Councillor Petty.

Councillor D. Graydon Petty: Madam Mayor, as usual Councillor Kingsford is a tough act to follow. I suppose I could, at this time, go back in the past and talk about ancestors. I'd rather not do that. I could refer to an article by Mrs. Burns: Do you remember when huge bonfires were lit in front of the homes of defeated candidates on election nights? I remember my mother carrying old wooden boxes to keep the bonfires going. I imagine Mr. Cowan [Keith, director of public works] would be quite pleased that this tradition is not carried on.

But as we proceed with some uncertainty into a different phase of regional government and try to forecast what the future will bring, let the great Kreskin reflect for a moment on the answers to a multitude of questions that I know many of you are asking.

And the first answer is "Ring around the tire." And of course the question is "What's the number one song at Goodyear?" I'll wait 'til some of these sink in; I choose not to be serious this evening.

The second answer is "Valerie Watkins." And the question, of course, is, "Who is the spine tickler?"

The third answer that has been plaguing one member of council. The answer is "If we have the bread, honey." And the question, of course, is "Will the festival be a success?"

The fourth answer is "A Booster." And the question is, "What do you need for a dead battery?"

The ... oops ... I have gesticulations for the next answer. And the question is often posed in that way by our reeve. The next answer is "a tie." And the question is, "What is three-three?"

Next answer: "King of the Road." Question: "What beats Queen of the Sidewalk?"

Next answer is "250 pounds." And the question, of course, is "What is hard to lose?"

Next answer: "The figure." Question: "Who has given us the financial facts?"

Next answer is "Bylaw." And the question, of course, is "What do you say when you leave a policeman?"

Next answer: "Sitting on the bench." The question is: "What beats sitting on the sidewalk?"

Although this evening we are saying "'bye" to the formal incorporation of a community, the mere change of political boundaries will never dampen the inner-spirit and dedication of its members. I have every reason to believe that the untiring efforts of the citizens of this community will continue to flourish and that the community spirit will endure for many years to come.

And in closing, I would like to perhaps reiterate what Councillor Kingsford has said so ably; that is, to add my own personal thanks to the many citizens for their involvement in this community—not only to those who served actively on boards and commissions, but for those who gave so untiringly of their efforts for the many good causes of this community.

To my fellow councillors, thank you for your indulgence on many occasions such as this one. I hope I'm not remembered just for Pettyisms. Even if I am, perhaps there's nothing too terribly wrong with that.

To our mayor, a special thanks for her guidance and direction throughout these past two years, and sincere wishes for the future. Madam mayor, you are ... and have given us very freely of your knowledge. I hope that this can also be given to members of the new city council, as I know it will be. To the staff, who often get nothing but bylaws, criticisms, and more work to do, thank you, personally, for the great deal of time, effort, and guidance that you have given to municipal matters—especially to us fledglings who, on many occasions, didn't know what we were talking about but tried to get across to the public the fact that we did; and you bailed us out on many occasions. And for that I am personally deeply, deeply grateful. That's all I have to say, Madam Mayor.

Mayor Hazel McCallion: Councillor Watkins.

Councillor J.L. Watkins: Thank you, Madam Mayor. Indeed, the acts are getting tougher to follow. I'm glad I'm not where Fred [Dineley] is sitting. Madam Mayor, members of council, and guests: On this New Year's Eve, 1973, the time-worn adage "Out with the old, in with the new" has a special meaning to this council. Hence, I attend this, the very final council meeting, with mixed feelings. Although I am somewhat saddened by the demise of our town in some four-and-a-half hours, it is indeed gratifying to know that the Ward of Streetsville can expect the best representation and leadership in the person of Her Worship Mayor, and soon to be promoted to Councillor, Hazel.

These past two years have been most significant, with many challenges and a few frustrations, too. However, I, for one, have thoroughly enjoyed working with a great council, and I thank you all for your support. Of course, no praise would be complete without a special vote of thanks to the staff, a fantastic staff. I do not believe there is a more dedicated, knowledgeable, or willing group of people anywhere, and I wish them well in their next posts.

If I were asked what was this council's greatest achievement these past two years, I believe I would say that it was the completion of Phase I of the downtown core. I am proud to have been contributory in one small way to this complex, and at times exasperating, project. However, I'm sure we all agree that having the finest core area in the new City of Mississauga justifies every penny, every meeting, and every frustration.

In summary, let me say that we have spent many hours here, and we have also spent a goodly amount of money. I trust we have been serious most of the time, and, occasionally, we have been able to have a good laugh, too. We have agreed on the majority of matters and yet we have had the fortitude to disagree on a few. In short, I believe we have been practising real democracy at a grassroots level.

May 1974 prove prosperous for each and every one of you and for all the citizens of Streetsville. And may our New Year's resolution be to carry into the new city that unique Streetsville spirit and civic-mindedness, which, in my opinion, is second to none. Happy New Year, everyone.

Councillor F.J. Dineley: Madam Mayor and members of council, town staff, and fellow residents: First, I want to thank you all for your help and co-operation during my first and, sadly, my only year on town council. This is probably the busiest year in Streetsville's history and certainly one of the most unique. In my opinion, it's provided us all with some invaluable experience.

When I was elected to office a little over a year ago, I never thought I would have the questionable distinction of being the last person ever elected to a Streetsville town council. Of course, this was before our town was arbitrarily eliminated. So tonight's last meeting is, for me, one of sadness, but not of regret, because I know that we did everything legally possible to retain and expand our cherished community.

In closing, I want to wish all the people of Streetsville a Happy New Year in 1974, and to Mayor McCallion I wish continued success on the council of the City of Mississauga, where she will represent us in her usual able manner. Thank you.

Mayor Hazel McCallion: Councillor Rea.

Councillor E.P. Rea: Madam Mayor, for fear of sounding like a parrot, my remarks are going to be very brief. I'd like to first of all thank the people of Streetsville again for giving me the opportunity of representing them in Ward 2. I'd like to thank the staff of the town for the advice and constructive criticism they've given us at times. And to you, Madam Mayor, I'd like to thank you for the patience and fairness and guidance that you've given us as young members of council over the last three or four years. If this council has been productive, I think a lot of the credit must go to you. Thank you.

Mayor Hazel McCallion: Councillor Spencer?

Councillor D.D. Spencer: Madam Mayor, fellow councillors, staff, and fellow citizens: Being last on the list, I think it's pretty well all been said. I would just like to say, again, thank you very much to the staff. I think they worked hard, they were co-operative, and they very rarely yelled at me.

The other "thank you" I would like to give is to the rest of this council. I would very personally like to thank you. We have fought a fair number of battles, and we have disagreed and agreed, but I always discovered that we could go out that door, and, almost invariably, that was the end. It was a battle fought, and it was won or lost, and we pressed on to the next one. And I'd like to thank you very, very much for the exercise in democracy and the fun and enjoyment of trying to be petty at something. Happy New Year and thank you.

Mayor Hazel McCallion: Deputy Reeve Graham.

Deputy Reeve J.S. Graham: Thank you, Madam Mayor. This is on a somewhat different note: I would like to go back a few years; at a Meet-the-Candidates Night in November 1969, as an acclaimed councillor, I likened Streetsville to a ship and made reference to all events and activities in nautical terms. Now the good ship "Streetsville" is in port and secured at Pier 9, her three-year tour of duty being shortened to two, on orders from the admiralty. Her officers and crew have performed admirably, and even the passengers willingly pitched in when their help was needed. As a result, we now have a trim ship with new fittings; a ship that is apparently the admiration and envy of others, near and far.

But the decommission papers have come through. The crew members have received their transfers, and the officers, with the exception of the captain, have been either retired or put on reserve. Captain McCallion will be an officer on the new ship "Mississauga", which will be taking its shake-down cruise immediately. We will all be aboard this new ship, and it will take the concerted effort of all those who are burdened with responsibilities to make it a safe, secure, and enjoyable cruise. The passengers will again be asked to stand by and help the officers and crew.

I trust that all those transferring at Pier 9 will perform in the commendable way that has won them so much admiration. Best wishes and smooth sailing.

Mayor Hazel McCallion: Now I'd like to call on our reeve, Bob Weylie.

Reeve R.M. Weylie: Thank you, Madam Mayor. Fellow members of council, members of staff, ladies and gentlemen: Everybody's said, "what a tough act to follow," and I've got a real tough one now.

Over the past six years on council, there have been many, many things that I remember, but I think one of the funniest occurrences that's happened here was about three or four years ago when we had a little problem with a street called Water Street in town. And at the time, there seemed to be a problem of surveys that differed, and as a result we didn't know where Water Street was. As a result, after the council meeting—after this was dealt with—one of the local papers printed a story, the headline reading "Council can't find Water Street"—and, of course, went on to explain what the problem was. About two days after the article was printed, I had a call from a resident telling me where Water Street was. So that's one that I think I'll remember for a long time.

Getting back to the more serious vein, I think that this particular time is a sad occasion, not one to look forward to. If we go back in history a little bit, Streetsville has a very long history in terms of municipalities in Canada or in Ontario. Streetsville was founded in the 1820s, it was incorporated as a village in 1858, became a town in 1962. Streetsville has been a leader in many, many ways during this period. I understand it had some of the first mills in the area; it certainly had some of the first bricks in the area, and we have, I believe, a house with one of the first brick walls built in this part of the country. I think Streetsville can be very proud of the people who led it. I refer not only to members of council through the years, but people on boards and committees, and, certainly, its citizens. Its citizens have always been willing to participate, whether it be on boards and committees, where many, many have done so voluntarily, or when it came to our stand against regional government. First of all, we had the SCORE campaign, and many, many people in Streetsville turned out and got petitions and forwarded them to the government to try and save our municipality. Then, when that one failed, the next was SPUR— Streetsville's Place Under Regionalism—again, another example of people trying to save their municipality and working and supporting the council and planning boards and the people who were involved.

In addition, I think we can all be very, very proud of the staff we've had in this municipality. We have one member of our staff who has been here some 23 years, I believe it is—our town clerk. He's done an excellent job over those entire 23 years. We have another gentleman sitting with us this evening who has been solicitor for some 20 years for the Town of Streetsville, or the Village of Streetsville as it was in those days. I think that any municipality which has a record of people such as that, plus the new members of staff who have come along since and added their expertise, can be very, very proud. And last, but not least, I would like to point out the contributions of the members of this council. I think it's probably one of the best councils this town has had. We've all worked well together, and I would like to say "thank you" to each and every one of you for your co-operation over the last few years; it's made the job very interesting and very easy to do. And our mayor, Hazel McCallion, has done an outstanding job of leading the council. Without her, we would not have gone the distance we have or done the things we have done. She's done a fantastic job, and I know that she will continue to do the same thing as our representative on the Mississauga council and on the regional council of Peel. And Hazel, my personal thanks to you, and my best wishes for the years that lie ahead.

Mayor Hazel McCallion: We have with us Judge Allen in the audience tonight, who was our solicitor for twenty-some years. Would you like to, from the bench, say a few words?

A Member of Council: Or the sidewalk!

Mayor Hazel McCallion: Or the sidewalk....

Judge H.W. Allen: Well, Madam Mayor and members of council, and friends of Streetsville: I've always felt a great attachment to this municipality. You received me as a new boy some twenty-odd years ago, and over that period I've enjoyed working with various councils and boards and commissions and the people of Streetsville. I think the unbiased expression of opinion ... I always felt that Streetsville played a part in the affairs of this general area, the County of Peel, in a way that was quite disproportionate to its size. I felt that your importance was greater than your size, and I hope that with Hazel still representing this area that that importance will continue to be felt in the new regional government. I certainly say thank you to members of council, past and present, and particularly to Mayor McCallion, all the very best for 1974.

Mayor Hazel McCallion: Now, our clerk who has served us for 23 years. He's been working so hard I don't think he possibly has the energy, but Len, would you like to give your last advice to council?

A Member of Council: I don't think I want to hear it!

Clerk-Administrator L.M. McGillivary: I would just like to wish council, members of council, all the best for the next year. At the same time, I would at this time like to sincerely extend my sincere appreciation to council for the gift which they gave me a few weeks ago. The holiday was certainly enjoyed by my wife and I; the only trouble is, you should have made it in January when I could take three weeks. The south was lovely.

Again, thank you very much. And I must thank you for the sizeable cheque which I received today in appreciation of our overtime.

Mayor Hazel McCallion: Thank you, Len. Emmaleen is our new treasurer; rather new to the municipality. Would you like to say a few words?

Treasurer E. Sabourin: It was totally unexpected, but Madam Mayor, members of council, on behalf of our staff in the general office, we'd like to say thank you to you people for the good relationship we've had over the past two years. There were times when you weren't exactly welcomed through the door. It was just a case where we were busy, and I'm glad you put up with us! We certainly wish each of you, personally, all the very best in the future. Thank you.

Mayor Hazel McCallion: I think, as all the members of council have expressed themselves so well in paying tribute to the citizens of Streetsville, I would like to pay tribute to the press—the local press—the *Streetsville Review* and any other press members that are here and have been there over the years. [They] have attempted to bring to the citizens of Streetsville the efforts of our council. There were times when we even disagreed with the press, members of council. But again, we seemed to come out on top, or they did—one or the other. But at least we informed the citizens.

I would like to, as my concluding remarks, just read what I said in front of the program for the recognition dinner—that the staff has served the citizens well. They have performed their duties with a concern for the people they have served. They have dealt efficiently, expeditiously, and sympathetically with the problems of the citizens and have gone beyond the call of duty. The citizens who have served on our boards and commissions have contributed freely of their time and talents to make this community great. They have taken the fate of their community into their own hands and have shaped its destiny. They have had a desire to serve their fellow citizens by placing at their disposal the fruits of their knowledge, the results of their studying, and the product of their talents.

From its very beginning, things have happened in Streetsville. The community has attained many firsts. Through the efforts of all, the beauty of the community has been enhanced; a community spirit second-to-none has existed. And even though tonight the Town of Streetsville as a municipal entity ceases to exist at midnight, I know that the spirit of the Town of Streetsville will carry on. It will play a major role in the development of the new City of Mississauga.

I'd like to say to the citizens and to the members of council, what a privilege it is for me to represent you at the new City of Mississauga. And I hope that very shortly, in the new year, we will be setting up a Streetsville Community Association that will truly represent the interests of the Town of Streetsville and will serve as an advisory group, a consulting group, or whatever we may call it, to assist me, especially with the great responsibility that I will assume as of midnight tonight as your representative of our community.

We have had so many people representing the interests and the concerns of the people of Streetsville, that you can rest assured that I certainly am very conscious of the responsibility that falls to me at midnight. I hope that the members of council will be always available and that I can call on them to assist me and that they will bring a line of communication to me. Because if you saw the schedule that was presented to us yesterday—or Friday—and today, I will not be spending many hours in the Town of Streetsville. The meetings are extensive, both day and evening. And so I am going to be looking for a real line of communication with the residents of Streetsville, and so that I will be, as I've tried to be in the past, close to my people. That is my wish for 1974—to be close to the people of Streetsville. I hope that you will help me to do this.

And so I will now pass on to the resolution which closes out our Town of Streetsville—the bylaw.

Reeve R.M. Weylie: Madam Mayor, I would move a short first reading of the bylaw to close out the municipality

Mayor Hazel McCallion: A seconder for the motion.

Deputy Reeve J.S. Graham: I second the motion.

Mayor Hazel McCallion: Any discussion? All in favour? Any opposed? Carried.

Clerk-Administrator L.M. McGillivary: A bylaw to close out the Corporation of the Town of Streetsville.

Reeve R.M. Weylie: Madam Mayor, I'd move a short second reading of the bylaw to close out the municipality.

Mayor Hazel McCallion: Seconder?

Deputy Reeve J.S. Graham: I second the motion.

Mayor Hazel McCallion: Any discussion? All in favour? Any opposed? Carried.

Clerk-Administrator L.M. McGillivary: A bylaw to close out the Corporation of the Town of Streetsville.

Reeve R.M. Weylie: Madam Mayor, I would move a long third reading of the bylaw.

Deputy Reeve J.S. Graham: I second the motion.

Mayor Hazel McCallion: Any discussion? Would you like to read it, Mr. Clerk? Or Mr. Reeve, would you like to read it?

Reeve R.M. Weylie: Thank you, Madam Mayor.

WHEREAS Streetsville was founded in 1820;

AND WHEREAS Streetsville was incorporated as a Village in 1858;

AND WHEREAS the Village of Streetsville was incorporated as a Town on January 1st, 1962.

AND WHEREAS by Bill 138, being an Act to establish the Regional Municipality of Peel, which was passed by the Legislature of the Province of Ontario on the 22nd day of June, 1973, the Corporation of the Town of Streetsville was amalgamated with the Town of Port Credit and a part of the Town of Mississauga was annexed thereto to form a new municipality to be known as the City of Mississauga as of January 1st, 1974.

NOW THEREFORE this Bylaw will confirm the actions of the municipal council for the Corporation of the Town of Streetsville during their tenure in office.

AND FURTHER this Bylaw will officially dissolve the municipal council of the Corporation of the Town of Streetsville.

This Bylaw shall become effective on the date of enactment by council.

Mayor Hazel McCallion: Any discussion on the resolution? I think somebody said tonight, "If you all voted against it, what would happen?"

All in favour? Any opposed? Carried.

I have a resolution moved by Deputy Reeve Graham, seconded by Councillor Watkins: "That the mayor's chain of office be presented to the Streetsville and District Chamber of Commerce, as it was this organization that donated this chain of office at the time that the Village of Streetsville was incorporated as a Town on January 1st, 1962."

I would now like to ask the president of the chamber of commerce to come forward and receive this, and I would like the president of the Streetsville Historical Society to come forward so ...

Mr. A. W. Betts: Mayor McCallion, on behalf of the Streetsville and District Chamber of Commerce, I accept the chain of office, which you have worn so well and which your predecessors have, too. And so that it will remain within our area as a reminder of what we have done in the past, I am going to hand it over now to the Streetsville Historical Society, so that they can take care of it for us.

Mrs. G. Williams: Thank you very much, and we do promise that we will take good care of it, and I do wish, on behalf of the historical society, to thank the members ... all of the members of council for their co-operation to our society, and I hope that from now on they'll be able to attend all our meetings.

Mayor Hazel McCallion: To the members of the audience: This chain of office will be duly placed in a glass cage—if that's the word for it—case, and will remain within the boundaries of the Town of Streetsville at all times. That is a condition on which it is turned over to the historical society.

Any discussion on the motion? All in favour? Any opposed? Carried.

A Member of the Audience: Madam Chairman, many years ago I presented the gavel to the Town of Streetsville. I was wondering what was going to happen with that?

Mayor Hazel McCallion: Is this the gavel?

A Member of the Audience: Yes.

Mayor Hazel McCallion: This is being turned over to the historical society. We hope that an appropriate plaque will be placed on it; there isn't one at the present time.

And to the members of council, just so that it's legal, I hope that ... I know that you will want to, and I know that we are only too happy to present you with your name plaque that is in front of you. There are no ashtrays to take here!

I would now like you all to stand. I think we should conclude the great Town of Streetsville, or the municipal entity as a town, with a prayer given by Deputy Reeve Graham at the recognition dinner, that I think many of you may not have heard. I think I would like you all to stand and join with me in this prayer:

A town, its people, their laughter and tears,
Their labour and leisure, their hopes and their fears.

A place to share this gift of living,
To become involved through an act of giving.

In a town, in a meeting, in a friendship, in a care,
Tonight we give thanks for these blessings we share.

And so, ladies and gentlemen, so ends the Municipal Corporation of the Town of Streetsville.

Motion to Adjourn? A seconder for the motion? All in favour?

Thank you all for coming!

Notes

All references to the Archives of Ontario's temporary boxes (tb) with the code RG 19-131 are to the document series labelled "West of Metro files." The documents were all generated in the late 1960s or early 1970s.

PREFACE

1. See, for example, Clarence N. Stone, "Urban Regimes and the Capacity to Govern: A Political Economy Approach," *Journal of Urban Affairs* 15:1 (1993).

2. The article appeared on October 1, 1997.

3. A few of the interviews were conducted for the author's *Booster* articles. The endnotes indicate where this is the case.

I attempted on many occasions to schedule an interview with the Honourable William Davis, premier of Ontario at the time of amalgamation and the member of provincial parliament for Peel North, which included Streetsville. After several postponements by Mr. Davis's office, we were finally due to meet on December 12, 2000, at Mr. Davis's law office in Toronto. When I arrived, I learned that Mr. Davis was not able to make it in because of the major snowstorm. That morning, Mr. Davis (still at home) and I had a short, pleasant telephone conversation, during which the former premier spoke of the South Peel Water and Sewage Scheme, describing it as an important event in the years preceding the creation of regional government. He also noted that he sometimes reminds Hazel McCallion that she would not have become the mayor of Mississauga had it not been for amalgamation.

The former premier agreed that his secretary would schedule an appointment shortly after Mr. Davis's return from an upcoming vacation, in order that we could have a more detailed discussion. Unfortunately, all my subsequent attempts to set up a time for a meeting were unsuccessful. The apparent reluctance may not be unusual. Mr. Davis's biographer, Claire Hoy, notes in his Acknowledgments section that he had difficulty getting an interview, although he was finally successful (*Bill Davis—A Biography.* Toronto: Methuen, 1985). We can only hope the former premier will decide to write his memoirs or prepare detailed recordings, so as to provide the people of Ontario with as full an account as possible of his time in public life, including his 14 years as first minister.

CHAPTER 1: STREETSVILLE, 1973

1. Stephen Leacock, *Sunshine Sketches of a Little Town* (Toronto: Bell and Cockburn, 1912), p. 1.

2. Streetsville's audited financial statements for the year ended December 31, 1972 (prepared by MacGillivray & Co.) put the town's population at the end of that year at 7,183. See "Streetsville Financial Statements" file in Region of Peel Archives, RG 1, 1994.063.070 AR, Box 5.

3. See, for example, James Lorimer, *The Developers* (Toronto: Lorimer, 1978), p. 43.

4. This statement was made to the author in an interview for the article "The year the people lost their town," *Booster*, October 1, 1997.

5. M.D. Lundy, *Memories of Early Days in Streetsville* (The *Streetsville Review*, 1957), p. 1. Region of Peel Archives, Mary Manning Collection, 1998.035, Series 4, File 5.

6. Al Betts, interview with the author, August 1999.

7. The letter is dated April 17, 1972. Archives of Ontario, RG 19-131, tb 8.

8. The program can be found in the Archives of the Streetsville Historical Society. This holding is not catalogued.

9. Streetsville Public Library Annual Reports, Region of Peel Archives, 1985.174 AR, Box 1, files 2-3.

10. Mary Manning, *A History of Streetsville* (Streetsville Historical Society, 1973), p. 14. There have been two subsequent revised editions of

this publication. The most recent (1990) has this reference on page 18. For another brief overview of Streetsville's history, see Manning, "Town of Streetsville," Chapter 32 in *A History of Peel County to Mark its Centenary as a Separate County* (Brampton: Peel County, 1967).

11. The organization frequently had short columns in the *Review* with advice to fellow residents.

12. See, for example, Tom Urbaniak, "For the love of gardening," *Booster*, May 17, 2001.

13. This is the mission statement of the society. It is prominently displayed on the cover of some of its publications.

14. Information on the town's clubs and associations can be found in the Promotional Committee file, Region of Peel Archives, 1994.063.070 AR, Box 5. Information on courses can be found in the recreation booklet, Parks and Recreation Board file, same location.

15. See, for example, "Town Council prepares for election," *Booster*, August 3, 1965.

16. Manning, *A History of Streetsville* (1990 edition), p. 18.

17. The letter is dated March 12, 1973. Archives of Ontario, RG 19-131, tb 8.

18. See, for example, Parks and Recreation Board file, Region of Peel Archives, 1994.063.070 AR, Box 5.

19. John Kernaghan, "Joe's fish market: business experiment in Streetsville core," *Mississauga Times*, November 14, 1973.

20. Joe Simoes, interview with the author, June 2001.

21. John Kernaghan, "Integrating Streetsville's Portuguese," *Mississauga Times*, September 29, 1971.

22. See, for example, the editor's response to a letter from Streetsville resident John Cheshire, *Booster*, August 3, 1965.

23. "Streetsville's nomination to be held November 22nd at Russell Langmaid School," *Booster*, November 2, 1965.

24. Planning Board Minutes, 1965-1966. Region of Peel Archives, 1996.065.025 AR, Box 5. For a good example of McCallion's frustration with the board, see the Minutes for September 13, 1965.

25. Hazel McCallion, interview with the author, August 1999.

26. Don Hewson, interview with the author, August 2000.

27. "Housing Freeze Back: Plan for 'Hub' Town," *Mississauga News*, November 29, 1967.

28. Minutes, March 4, 1968, Region of Peel Archives, 1994.063, Box 3.

29. Minutes, June 3, 1968, Region of Peel Archives, 1994.063, Box 3.

30. It appears that at the July 15, 1968, meeting of town council, Graham was finally left standing alone when the other members of council voted to approve a settlement recommended by General Committee 1. See Minutes, Region of Peel Archives, 1994.063, Box 3. The issue was on council and committee agendas throughout the spring and summer. For information on the fence dispute see, for example, "'Don't fence us in,' say lawnbowlers," *Review*, May 29, 1968, and "Lawnbowlers retain new lawyer," *Review*, June 19, 1968. See also Tom Urbaniak, "A sport for everyone: Inside the Streetsville Lawn Bowling Club," *Booster*, July 26, 2001.

31. This issue was dealt with at the January 6, 1969, meeting of council. The Minutes are at the Region of Peel Archives, 1994.063, Box 3.

32. See, for example, "Lull before the storm as civic leaders clash," *South Peel Weekly*, January 15, 1969.

33. "SRA accepts Plunkett Report, Town Council rejects it," *Booster*, December 6, 1966.

34. See, for example, "Regional Government," *Booster*, July 3, 1968.

35. Committee of the Whole Report, July 15, 1968. Region of Peel Archives, 1994.063, Box 3.

36. "Streetsville Council meets to discuss regional government," *Review*, July 10, 1968.

37. "Streetsville mayor to quit, assails amalgamation foes," *Toronto Star*, October 1, 1969.

38. See, for example, Bob Cooper, *County to Keystone – Reflections of Peel, 1974-99* (Brampton: Regional Municipality of Peel, 2000), p. 20.

39. An example of the board's harsh reaction to the matter can be found in a letter to council from Chairman F.J. McDonnell, April 4, 1966, in "Newsclippings and Correspondence" file, Streetsville Public Library Documents, Region of Peel Archives, 1985.174 AR, Box 1.

40. *Building Program for Centennial Public Library in Streetsville*, 2nd Draft, in "Newsclippings and Correspondence" file, Streetsville Public Library Documents, Region of Peel Archives, 1985.174 AR, Box 1.

41. *Mississauga Times*, January 3, 1973 (untitled).

42. James MacGregor Burns, *Leadership* (New York: Harper and Rowe, 1978), p. 40.

43. "What's owed from an MP," *Booster*, August 3, 1965.

44. P.T. Rooke and R.L. Schnell, *No Bleeding Heart: Charlotte Whitton, A Feminist on the Right* (Vancouver: University of British Columbia Press, 1987).

45. These remarks appear in Tom Urbaniak, "Dowling down memory lane," *Booster*, June 25, 1997.

46. *Return of Elected and Appointed Officers of a Local Municipality for the year 1971*, Region of Peel Archives, Clerk's Files, 1973, RG 1, 1994.063 AR, Box 5.

47. Winifred McGillivary, interview with the author, June 1998.

48. Linda Evans, interview with the author, August 2000.

49. Doug Spencer, interview with the author, August 1998.

50. Information about credentials and the professional development activities of Streetsville's employees can be found in the *Submission by the Corporation of the Town of Streetsville on Proposed Municipal Reorganization in Peel County*, March 28, 1973, in Streetsville Clerk's Files, 1973, Region of Peel Archives, RG 1, 1994.063.070 AR, Box 5. See also Archives of Ontario, RG 19-131, tb 7.

51. These details can be found in McGillivray and Company's audited financial statements for the Town of Streetsville for the year ended December 31, 1972. "Streetsville Financial Statements" file, Region of Peel Archives, 1994.063.070 AR, Box 5.

52. "Taxes reduced," *Booster*, May 2, 1972. See also, "Streetsville holds tax line," *Booster*, May 30, 1973; and "Streetsville holds the tax line in 1973," *Review*, May 30, 1973. The assumption that the average ratepayer saw no increase can also be made because overall revenues from taxation grew only marginally in 1973 over 1972. See the 1972 audited financial statements, *op. cit.*

53. Fletcher's comments were made in an interview with the author, September 1999.

54. Eric Ladner, interview with the author, August 2000.

55. "Chief Fletcher favors regional police force," *Mississauga News*, March 8, 1972.

56. Report of Chief D.E. Fletcher to E.P. Rea, chairman, Streetsville Police Committee, December 8, 1972, in "Streetsville Police Department" file, Region of Peel Archives, RG 1, 1994.063.070 AR, Box 5.

57. Some of the more common bylaws are highlighted in the Promotional Committee folder, Region of Peel Archives, RG 1, 94.063.070 AR, Box 5. For more information on the bicycle licensing bylaw, see "Streetsville okays $1 licence for bikes," *Toronto Star*, June 27, 1972.

58. The interviews with the former firefighters were conducted by the author for a *Booster* article, "Looking back at the Streetsville Volunteer Fire Department," August 5, 1998.

59. Tweedsmuir Committee of the Streetsville's Women's Institute, *Through a Century with Streetsville* (*Streetsville Review*, 1959), p. 79.

60. "Man dies – home gutted – boiler explodes," *Review*, December 28, 1973.

61. "New day care centre in Streetsville makes 880 in Ontario," *Toronto Star*, October 27, 1972.

62. Ontario. Niagara Region Local Government Review. *Report* (Toronto: Department of Municipal Affairs, 1966), p. 67.

63. Mary Manning, "Speech to the University Women's Club, Mississauga," April 10, 1997. Region of Peel Archives, Mary Manning Collection, 1998.035, Series 1, Box 4, File 13.

64. As the "Librarian's Report" for 1972 stated, "So it is indeed true that our patrons have access to books from all over Canada." Region of Peel Archives, RG 1, 1985.0174, Box 1.

65. Elizabeth Colley, interview with the author, July 2000.

66. Library Board Minutes, January 16, 1973, Region of Peel Archives, RG 1, 1985.0174, Box 1.

67. Details on the history of the PUC can be found in a short, untitled Ontario Hydro document at the Region of Peel Archives, RG 1, 1987.043, Box 13.

68. See, for example, "5 municipalities reach agreement after 3 days," *Review*, March 13, 1968.

69. See, for example, "Billion dollar plan will attract 200,000 to Mississauga area," *South Peel Weekly*, April 30, 1969.

70. John Wiersma, interview with the author, August 1999.

71. Wiersma interview.

72. "June is Hydro month," *Booster*, June 1, 1972.

73. Ron Walker, interview with the author, August 1999.

74. For example, the preamble to By-law #1 of the Parks and Recreation Board (legally still referred to as the "Board of Park Management of the Town of Streetsville") stated:

WHEREAS by Subsection I of Section II of the Public Parks Act (R.S.O. 1970, c. 384, as amended) authority is given to Parks Boards to pass by-laws for the use, regulation, protection and government of the parks, avenues, boulevards, and drives, the approaches thereto, and streets connecting the same, not inconsistent with the Public Parks Act or any law of Ontario.... (Region of Peel Archives, Parks and Recreation Board 1973 files, 1994.063 AR, Box 5).

75. R. Mispel-Beyer, director of recreation for the Town of Streetsville, to E.M. Halliday, parks and recreation commissioner, Town of Mississauga (July 6, 1973), in Region of Peel Archives, Parks and Recreation Board 1973 files, 1994.063 AR, Box 5.

76. Town of Streetsville, *Parks and Recreation Summer Programs, 1973,* in Region of Peel Archives, Parks and Recreation Board 1973 files, 1994.063 AR, Box 5.

77. Ralph Hunter, interview with the author, October 1999.

78. Mispel-Beyer to Halliday, *op. cit.*

79. Jim Robinson, "Beehoo Industries faces shut-down, Streetsville economy debate builds," *Mississauga News*, February 10, 1971.

80. A 10-year perspective of the town's finances can be found in McGillivray and Co., *Corporation of the Town of Streetsville – Financial Report for the Year Ended December 31, 1972,* in "Streetsville Financial Statements" file, Region of Peel Archives, RG 1, 1994.063.070 AR, Box 5.

81. These questions were formulated at a special joint meeting of council and the planning board held on June 3, 1969. The Minutes are at

the Region of Peel Archives, 1994.063 AR, Box 3.

82. This statement was made on December 11, 1972. It is included as an appendix to Streetsville's official response (March 28, 1973) to the January 1973 provincial proposals for regional government. Streetsville Clerk's Files, 1973, Region of Peel Archives, RG 1, 1994.063.070 AR, Box 5. See also Archives of Ontario, RG 19-131, tb 7.

83. See John Sewell, *Up Against City Hall* (Toronto: James, Lewis and Samuel, 1972).

84. The article, "Confessions of a City Hall Clubman," which appeared in the Toronto reformers' newspaper *City Hall* (April 1970), is reprinted in *Inside City Hall: The Year of the Opposition* (Toronto: Hakkert, 1971).

85. It is included in the same appendix as the policy statement, *op. cit.*

86. "What or Who," *Booster*, June 7, 1966.

87. A case in point is the *Booster*'s ongoing 1971 coverage of the new Meadowvale community, especially the portion that was being built within Streetsville's boundaries. The articles are not at all hostile, and give the impression that the mayor and town officials had established a working relationship with Markborough officials.

88. The new policies and the new emphasis are evident in the council and committee minutes from 1968. Region of Peel Archives, 1994.063, Box 3.

89. "Population up 10 percent, high rise units triple," *Mississauga Times*, June 19, 1974.

90. "Mississauga ignores engineer's warning, approves housing plan," *Toronto Star*, January 8, 1970.

91. John Beaufoy, "2 towns don't want to be part of Mississauga's growth," *Globe and Mail*, November 30, 1972.

92. Arthur Lowe, "New town outmatches even founders' dream," *Mississauga News*, January 24, 1968.

93. Phil Gibson, "Erin Mills, Meadowvale: What will they do to Mississauga?" *Mississauga News*, June 25, 1969.

94. "Streetsville's Folly," *Mississauga Times*, May 27, 1970.

95. "Feeding frenzy," *Mississauga Times*, July 5, 1972.

96. "Local autonomy is a myth," *Mississauga Times*, December 20, 1972.

97. An excerpt of McLuhan's comments is included on the inside cover of David and Nadine Nowlan, *The Bad Trip: The Untold Story of the Spadina Expressway* (Toronto: New Press—House of Anansi, 1970).

98. Rudy Platiel, "Streetsville fights for survival," *Globe and Mail*, April 21, 1972.

CHAPTER 2: THE REGIONAL GOVERNMENT QUESTION

1. Rudy Platiel, "Plan for 3 regions to west of Metro greeted with boos," *Globe and Mail*, January 24, 1973.

2. Ian Urquhart, "Regional government – No wonder the politicians protest," *Toronto Star*, January 24, 1973.

3. "Need for Solomon's touch," *Globe and Mail*, January 26, 1973.

4. For a good summary of the origins of local government institutions in Ontario, see C. Richard Tindal and Susan Nobes Tindal, *Local Government in Canada*—5th edition (Scarborough: Nelson, 2000), pp. 28-34.

5. See, for example, Katherine A. Graham et al., *Urban Governance in Canada: Representation, Resources and Restructuring* (Toronto: Harcourt Brace, 1998), pp. 172-173.

6. For an excellent comparative discussion of municipal amalgamations in Canada, the United States, and around the world, as well as a critique of recent forced municipal mergers in Canada, see Andrew Sancton, *Merger Mania: The Assault on Local Government* (Montreal: McGill-Queen's University Press, 2000).

7. *Report of the Royal Commission on Local Government in England, Volume 1.* (The Radcliffe-Maud Report) (London: H.M. Stationary Office, 1969), p. 10.

8. See, for example, Clarke Morrison, *Growth of a City: Mississauga, 1930-1974.* This short report was prepared for the Mississauga Judicial Inquiry in 1975 (Canadiana Room, Mississauga Central Library).

9. "Unique Study Result, Warning Neighbors," *Port Credit Weekly*, September 25, 1958.

10. "'Little Metro' meet flops," *Toronto Township News*, June 1, 1961.

11. Reprinted in *South Peel Weekly*, November 23, 1961. (The study is dated November 13, 1961.)

12. *Peel-Halton Local Government Review: A Report* (Toronto: Department of Municipal Affairs, 1966), p. 50.

13. "Report Study Awaited," *South Peel Weekly*, October 5, 1966.

14. Ontario Committee on Taxation, *Report, Vol. 1* (Toronto: Queen's Printer, 1967), p. 50.

15. A good, accurate summary of the provincial rationale for regional government can be found in the March 1973 brief to the provincial government prepared by the Peel Association for Good Government (PAGG). Archives of Ontario, RG 19-131, tb 6.

16. For a summary of the work of MTARTS and maps of the Goals Plans, see Richard Thoman, *Design for Development in Ontario: The Initiation of a Regional Planning Program* (Toronto, 1971).

17. Municipal Planning Consultants et al., *Town of Streetsville Boundary Study* (1968). A copy of the study can be found in the Streetsville Historical Society Archives and at the Erindale College Library (University of Toronto).

18. See, for example, "Mississauga is 'Big Daddy' as Peel and Halton joined in McKeough's New Metro," *South Peel Weekly*, January 22, 1969.

19. "McCallion: Streetsville fears Mississauga urban sprawl," *Mississauga Times*, February 18, 1970.

20. Archives of Ontario, RG 19-131, tb 8. The Mississauga clerk was G. Lumiss.

21. Letter from Darcy McKeough to H.H. Rutherford, clerk of Peel County, November 6, 1969, "Regional Government 1970" file, Region of Peel Archives, 1990.092 AR, Box 41.

22. McKeough's March 16, 1970, address to the Bolton Rotary Club can be found in the Region of Peel Archives, "Regional Government 1969" file, 1990.092, AR, Box 41.

23. See, for example, Mike Solomon, "New region proposes Streetsville, Mississauga cities," *Mississauga News*, May 6, 1970.

24. "Regional Government 1970" file, Region of Peel Archives, 1990.092 AR, Box 41.

25. "Mississauga land 'safe,'" *Toronto Star*, May 13, 1970.

26. "Metro approves Erin Mills, Streetsville charge overruled," *Mississauga Times*, May 27, 1970. See also "Metro okays Streetsville project to house 300,000," *Toronto Star*, May 21, 1970. The "Metro" reference is to the Metropolitan Toronto Planning Board.

27. Archives of Ontario, RG 19-131, tb 8.

28. Archives of Ontario, RG 19-131, tb 14.

29. See, for example, "Resentment high over regionalism," *Booster*, April 7, 1970.

30. A.K. McDougall, *John P. Robarts: His Life and Government*. (Toronto: University of Toronto Press, 1986), p. 229.

31. See, for example, "Peel-Halton merger scrapped; Mississauga presses city move," *Mississauga Times*, March 18, 1970.

32. The formal application was dated June 10, 1970. Archives of Ontario, RG 19-131, tb 7.

33. Dennis Anderson, "Trust is lacking between Mississauga and its neighbors," *Globe and Mail*, March 30, 1970.

34. Frank Calleja, "Debate heats up over amalgamation in Mississauga," *Toronto Star*, April 6, 1971.

35. See, for example, Mike Solomon, "City bid official!" *Mississauga News*, March 11, 1970; "Council passes annexation bylaw: Streetsville's reply to city bid," *Mississauga News*, March 11, 1970; "Mississauga Council takes action to gain city status from O.M.B," *Mississauga Times*, March 11, 1970; and "First Streetsville – Everybody on Annexation Kick – Then Mississauga," *Review*, March 25, 1970. See also the file entitled "By-law annexing Town of Streetsville," Region of Peel Archives, 1996.065, Box 4.

36. Archives of Ontario, RG 19-131, tb 8.

37. Sam Clasky to McKeough (January 4, 1971). Archives of Ontario, RG 19-131, tb 8.

38. The memorandum is dated September 11, 1970. Archives of Ontario, RG 19-131, tb 8.

39. The undated document is in the Archives of Ontario, RG 19-131, tb 8.

40. "County split feared over regional gov't," *Mississauga Times*, March 11, 1970.

41. "Regional government," *Booster*, April 6, 1971.

42. The monthly reports of the Municipal Organization Committee are in Peel County's bound annual volumes containing minutes, bylaws and official reports (Region of Peel Archives).

43. Many articles in the local press described SCORE's efforts. For a good summary of the campaign, see Rudy Platiel, "Streetsville fights for survival," *Globe and Mail*, April 21, 1972. See also Blake Goodings, "SCORE," *Booster*, April 5, 1972.

44. "Statement by the Honourable Darcy McKeough, Treasurer of Ontario, to the Founding Convention of the Association of Municipalities of Ontario," June 19, 1972, in *Design for Development—Phase Three* (Toronto: Queen's Printer, 1972), p. 12.

45. *Ibid.*, p. 10.

46. Davis interview on CHIC Radio, June 2, 1972. Archives of Ontario, Clare Westcott recordings, F 2094-8-0-40.

47. Darcy McKeough, interview with the author, July 2000.

48. Memorandum from J. Gardner Church, regional studies officer, to Ron Farrow, director, Local Government Organization Branch, July 7, 1972. Archives of Ontario, RG 19-131, tb 6.

49. This list of alternatives is in the Archives of Ontario, RG 19-131, tb 14.

50. *Report on Local Government Reform East and West of Metro to Policy and Priorities Board* (August 16, 1972), p. 20. Archives of Ontario, RG 19-131, tb 14.

51. *Ibid.*, p. 27.

52. County of Peel, *Submission on Municipal Reorganization to the Ministry of Treasury, Economics and Intergovernmental Affairs*, September 7, 1972. Region of Peel Archives, 1990.092 AR, Box 41.

53. See, for example, "Region Plan paper approved," *Mississauga Times*, August 30, 1972.

54. "Streetsville mayor wants provincial decision on region," *Toronto Star*, September 11, 1972.

55. *Submission to Cabinet on Local Government Organization in Peel* (December 1972), p. 27. Archives of Ontario, RG 19-131, tb 14.

CHAPTER 3: STREETSVILLE FIGHTS BACK

1. This front-page headline appeared on January 31, 1973.

2. "Mississauga happy, Streetsville angry," *Mississauga Times*, January 31, 1973; "Port Credit Council holds secret debate," *Mississauga News*, January 31, 1973. This article mentions Saddington's advocacy of an expanded Port Credit encompassing the lands south of the QEW. See also "Port Credit drops region fight, wants ward status," *Mississauga Times*, February 7, 1973.

3. A good summary of Port Credit's woes is in Frank Touby's article "Write On!", *Mississauga Times*, January 3, 1973.

4. John Beaufoy, "2 towns don't want to be part of Mississauga's growth," *Globe and Mail*, November 30, 1972.

5. Rudy Platiel, "Plan for 3 regions west of Metro greeted with boos," *Globe and Mail*, January 24, 1973.

6. "Reactions to regional government proposals run gamut of emotions," *Mississauga Times*, January 31, 1973.

7. Among these are the *Report to the Policy and Priorities Board* (August 1972) and the *Submission to Cabinet* (December 1972), Archives of Ontario, RG 19-131, tb 14.

8. Archives of Ontario, RG 19-131, tb 11.

9. The letter quoted a council resolution. It was signed by Mississauga deputy clerk David Turcotte and addressed to H.H. Rutherford, the clerk-treasurer of Peel County; "Municipal Re-organization 1972 (August-December)" file, Region of Peel Archives, 1990.092 AR, Box 41.

10. Ron Farrow, interview with the author, June 2000.

11. See especially the debates in the legislative assembly on the *Regional Municipality of Peel Act*, in *Hansard*, June 18, 1973 (pp. 3335-3378) and June 21, 1973 (pp. 3709-3739).

12. Peel Liaison Committee, Urban Development Institute, *Regional Government in Peel: A Response to the Provincial Government's Proposals* (no date), Archives of Ontario, RG 19-131, tb 6.

13. These letters and others from the developers are in the Archives of Ontario, RG 19-131, tb 6.

14. Archives of Ontario, RG 19-131, tb 8.

15. "McCallion: Streetsville fears Mississauga urban sprawl," *Mississauga Times*, February 19, 1970.

16. Darcy McKeough, interview with the author, July 2000.

17. The document is dated April 16, 1973. Archives of Ontario, RG 19-131, tb 6.

18. These comments appear on p. 5 of his remarks. Archives of Ontario, RG 19-131, tb 9.

19. David Allen, "Davis in own town, defends region plan," *Toronto Star*, January 25, 1973.

20. "Davis says criticism expected, indicates negotiations possible," *Globe and Mail*, January 25, 1973.

21. "Mississauga happy, Streetsville angry," *Mississauga Times*, January 31, 1973.

22. Jack Graham, interview with the author, June 2001.

23. Gianna Williams, "In My Opinion," *Review*, January 31, 1973.

24. "Letter from P.U.C.," *Review*, February 7, 1973.

25. These remarks are on p. 11 of Meen's speaking notes. Archives of Ontario, RG 3-49, tb 39, Range A, Davis General Correspondence, 1973.

26. Archives of Ontario, RG 3-49, tb 38, Range B, Davis General Correspondence, 1973.

27. Vic Dale, interview with the author, July 2000.

28. "Regional policy misunderstood," editorial in *London Free Press*, April 13, 1973.

29. The letter is dated March 27, 1972. Archives of Ontario, RG 19-131, tb 8.

30. "Mayor opens referendum information centre," *Review*, February 28, 1973.

31. The letter is dated February 28, 1973. It invites the provincial government "to display any data or information they feel would be bene-

ficial and helpful to bring about a better understanding of regional government." Archives of Ontario, RG 19-131, tb 7.

32. For descriptions of Meen's meeting with council, see, for example, "Meen visits Streetsville, holds closed door meeting," *Mississauga News*, February 14, 1973; and Hazel McCallion's letter to John White, April 2, 1973, Archives of Ontario, RG 19-131, tb 6.

33. Ron Farrow, interview with the author, June 2000.

34. "Now is the time to fight!" *Review*, February 21, 1973.

35. "To all residents of Streetsville – From SPUR Citizen's [sic] Action Committee," *Booster*, March 6, 1973.

36. This letter is reprinted in the *Booster,* March 6, 1973.

37. The petition is printed in the *Booster*, March 6, 1973.

38. Hyland's letter is dated March 6, 1973. Archives of Ontario, RG 19-131, tb 7.

39. Mary Manning to Premier Bill Davis, March 1, 1973. Archives of Ontario, RG 19-131, tb 7.

40. "Peel ignores 'railroading' charge, backs region plan," *Mississauga Times*, February 21, 1973.

41. The Peel brief is dated March 27, 1973. Archives of Ontario, RG 19-131, tb 6.

42. Norma Lynes, interview with the author, August 1998.

43. Archives of Ontario, RG 3-49, tb 9, Davis General Correspondence, 1973.

44. These arguments are on page 3 of the Mississauga brief in "Referendum re future status of town, 1973" file, Region of Peel Archives, 1994.963.070 AR, Box 5. Emphasis in the original.

45. The text of the ruling as well as other documents related to the case are in the Archives of Ontario, RG 37-6, OMB case files, File M7346. See also "OMB says no – Streetsville appeals to Cabinet," *Review*, March 14, 1973.

46. "We're darn mad, Bill Davis," *Review*, March 14, 1973.

47. Hazel McCallion, interview with the author, August 1999.

48. Bob Keeping, interview with the author, August 1999.

49. *Submission by the Corporation of the Town of Streetsville on Proposed Municipal Reorganization in Peel County*, March 28, 1973. Archives of Ontario, RG 19-131, tb 7. See also Streetsville clerk's files, 1973, Region of Peel Archives, 1994.063.070 AR, Box 5.

50. "Region will create higher taxes," *Mississauga Times*, April 4, 1973.

51. The letter is dated April 2, 1973. Archives of Ontario, RG 19-131, tb 6.

52. See, for example, White's letter to James Gray, February 28, 1973, Archives of Ontario, RG 50-1, tb 24, Minister's Correspondence files, 1973. The letter states, "The formation of a separate Streetsville municipality involving underdeveloped or rural lands would do nothing to alter the representation difficulties that you see in Peel."

53. These remarks are on pages 12-13 of the Mississauga report, *Comments Regarding the Submission by the Corporation of the Town of Streetsville on Proposed Municipal Reorganization in Peel* (April 13, 1973). Archives of Ontario, RG 19-131, tb 7.

54. "Bill Hamilton retires," *Booster*, August 10, 1971.

55. Graham's correspondence and Meen's letter to Davis, as well as Davis's note to his staff declining a meeting with Graham, are in the Archives of Ontario, RG 3-49, tb 39, Range B, Davis General Correspondence, 1973.

56. "Referendum refused but Streetsville still fights merger," *Toronto Star*, March 12, 1973. See also Blake Goodings, "A letter to residents," Booster, May 2, 1972. Goodings wrote that 2,781 out of 3,147 signatures were from Streetsville proper.

57. Archives of Ontario, RG 3-49, tb 9, Davis General Correspondence, 1973.

58. *Ibid.*

59. Graham interview.

60. Desmond Morton, *Mayor Howland: The Citizens' Candidate* (Toronto: Hakkert, 1973).

61. Morton, "Regional Government: The Prospect for Peel," *Erindalian*, February 27, 1973. The same article expresses some doubt about the determination of Streetsville's citizens. Subsequent articles by Morton were, however, much more emphatic about the strong activist impulse among the town's population.

62. Morton, "Politicians, powerful developers obstructed region," *Mississauga Times*, April 4, 1973.

63. Morton, interview with the author, August 2000.

64. The notes from the forum are in the Archives of Ontario, RG 19-131, tb 6.

65. See especially page 6 of the association's brief, Archives of Ontario, RG 19-131, tb 6.

66. A copy of this resolution is in the Archives of Ontario, RG 19-131, tb 7.

67. "White says decision on new Peel Region will not be delayed," *Toronto Star*, May 23, 1973.

68. The interview (with host Fraser Kelly) is in transcript form, Archives of Ontario, F 4151, tb 79, tr #81-982, John White papers.

69. The undated document is in the Archives of Ontario, RG 19-131, tb 6.

70. Archives of Ontario, RG 19-131, tb 6.

71. See p. 3 of the submission. Archives of Ontario, RG 19-131, tb 6.

72. Farrow interview.

73. Hazel McCallion, interview with the author, August 1999.

74. Farrow interview.

75. Archives of Ontario, RG 50-1, tb 28, Minister's Correspondence, 1973.

76. The speech was given in Hamilton on February 4, 1974. Archives of Ontario, RG 3-49, tb 34, Range A, Davis General Correspondence, 1974.

77. John White to Ken Cameron, August 17, 1973. Archives of Ontario, F 4151, tb 81, John White papers.

78. Harold G. Shipp to Premier Bill Davis, November 8, 1974. Archives of Ontario, RG 3-49, tr #18-969, Davis General Correspondence, 1974.

79. Meen's statement is in the Archives of Ontario, RG 19-131, tb 9.

80. McCallion to White, May 29, 1973. Archives of Ontario, RG 19-131, tb 7.

81. This sign, which was already up a few weeks earlier, is shown in

a *Toronto Star* photograph accompanying the article "Angry Streetsville to Davis: Resign," May 29, 1973.

82. For descriptions of Davis's appearance in Streetsville, see, for example, "Premier loudly booed by Streetsville crowd," *Globe and Mail*, June 15, 1973; and "Streetsville residents boo Davis over merger with Mississauga," *Toronto Star*, June 15, 1973.

83. See especially page 4 of the announcement. Archives of Ontario, RG 3-49, tb 34, Range A, Davis General Correspondence, 1974.

84. "Parkway belt plan backs Streetsville's stand says reeve," *Toronto Star*, June 6, 1973.

85. Norah Busby, interview with the author, July 2000.

86. Legislative Assembly of Ontario, *Hansard*, June 18, 1973, p. 3351.

87. E.L. Hoople, "Letter to the Editor: Town with a Heart," *Review*, October 31, 1973.

88. *Hansard, op. cit.*, p. 3356; see also p. 3359, where the speaker expresses concerns about Cassidy's "allegations."

89. *Ibid.*, p. 3355.

90. *Ibid.*, p. 3360.

91. Doug Kennedy, interview with the author, July 2000.

92. *Hansard*, June 21, 1973, p. 3715.

93. *Ibid.*, p. 3712.

CHAPTER 4: THE LAND OF BREAD AND HONEY

1. "Founders' Bread and Honey Festival a huge success," *Review*, June 6, 1973.

2. Guest was interviewed by the author in preparation for the article "Bread and Honey – A look back at a festival that grew," *Booster*, May 27, 1998.

3. Al Macdonald, interview with the author, May 1998.

4. The events of Bread and Honey weekend were widely reported in the Streetsville and Mississauga press. See also the "Promotional Committee" file, Region of Peel Archives, 1994.063 AR, Box 5.

5. See the advertisement in the *Review*, May 30, 1973.

6. Claudia Haddon, interview with the author for the article "Bread and Honey—A look back at a festival that grew," *Booster*, May 27, 1998.

7. Al Betts, interview with the author, August 1999.

8. *Review*, May 30, 1973.

9. Sylvia Weylie, interview with the author for the article "Bread and Honey—A look back at a festival that grew," *Booster*, May 27, 1998.

10. The Minutes are kept on file in the Streetsville Historical Society Archives.

11. Minutes of the Streetsville Public Library Board, March 29, 1973. Region of Peel Archives, RG 1, 1985.074, Box 1.

12. Descriptions of the proceedings and decisions of organizational meetings can be found in the records of the Promotional Committee, Region of Peel Archives, 1994.063 AR, Box 5.

13. Graham shared his reflections with the author in interviews held in May 1998 and July 2000.

14. Report of General Committee 1, December 14, 1972, Town of Streetsville Committee Reports – 1972, Region of Peel Archives, 1994.063, Box 3.

15. There are conflicting opinions on who suggested the name. Some interviewees recall that it was Sylvia Weylie. Others say that it was former mayor Bill Tolton. Still others insist that it emerged from no one in particular; that it was simply the result of collective brainstorming.

16. Promotional Committee file, Region of Peel Archives, 1994.063 AR, Box 5.

17. Parks and Recreation Board, Minutes of the meeting held on February 21, 1973. Region of Peel Archives, Town of Streetsville Committee Reports – 1973, 1994.063, Box 3.

18. Promotional Committee Report to Council, March 22, 1973. Region of Peel Archives, Town of Streetsville Committee Reports – 1973, 1994.063, Box 3.

19. "Co-ordinator needed for festival," *Review*, March 21, 1973.

20. Ted Russell, interview with the author for the article "Bread and Honey – A look back at a festival that grew," *Booster,* May 27, 1998.

CHAPTER 5: REVITALIZING DOWNTOWN STREETSVILLE

1. "Decay, blight," *Booster*, June 7, 1966.

2. 1968 Streetsville Council Minutes, Region of Peel Archives, 1994.063, Box 3.

3. "Core study unveiled," *Booster*, August 1, 1972.

4. "Saving atmosphere of old Streetsville," *Toronto Star*, July 26, 1972.

5. For an account of the extraordinary community-wide effort that went into constructing the cenotaph, see Streetsville Historical Society, *The Streetsville Cenotaph: A Village Memorial* (1992). See also Tom Urbaniak, "Caring for our Cenotaph," *Booster*, November 15, 2001.

6. "Streetsville blocks Bell Telephone work," *Toronto Star*, September 8, 1972.

7. Ralph Hunter, interview with the author, October 1999.

8. Eric Ladner, interview with the author, August 2000.

9. See, for example, Frank Florio, "Streetsville may retain students to help re-design downtown core," *Mississauga News*, February 7, 1973.

10. "Streetsville helps itself," *Mississauga Times*, February 7, 1973.

11. "Streetsville officials 'excited' by town core plan," *Mississauga Times*, February 7, 1973.

12. Report of General Committee 2, June 26, 1973, in Town of Streetsville Committee Reports—1973 files, Region of Peel Archives, 1994.063, Box 3. The town budget approved that spring allocated $60,000 to town core improvements. "Streetsville holds line on taxes," *Booster*, May 30, 1973.

13. See Watkins' comments in this book's appendix. Watkins also expressed this opinion when he was interviewed by the author (August 1999).

14. *Core '73 – A Downtown Rehabilitation Program*, p. 4. (This is the final report of the Core '73 group, released in January 1974; copy courtesy of Doug Flowers.)

15. *Ibid.*, p. 5.

16. Doug Flowers, interview with the author, June 1999. An article in the *Review* on September 19, 1973 ("Innovative sidewalks are subject of growing interest"), discussed this aspect of the work of Core '73.

17. The Minutes of these meetings are included with the 1973 Town of Streetsville Committee Reports, Region of Peel Archives, 1994.063, Box 3; see especially the Minutes for the meeting of June 29, 1973.

18. Peter Mah, interview with the author, September 2000.

19. See, for example, *Core '73*, p. 45.

20. "Core '73 dressing up Downtown Streetsville," *Mississauga Times*, May 30, 1973.

21. "Streetsville core plan working well: Flowers," *Mississauga News*, October 3, 1973.

22. The letter is reproduced on p. 23 of the *Core '73* report.

23. *Ibid.*, p. 22.

24. See pp. 30-49 of the *Core '73* report.

CHAPTER 6: ELECTING THE FIRST CITY COUNCIL

1. In fact, there were reports that Murray had turned his back on tradition by not appearing at all. See, for example, "Murray fails to show," *Review*, October 3, 1973.

2. For an excellent description of Murray's concession speech, see "Murray backers blink in disbelief," *Mississauga Times*, October 3, 1973.

3. See, for example,"Dobkin attacks town development policies," *Mississauga News*, July 11, 1973. For Murray's comments about "incremental growth," see *Brief to the Honourable Gordon Carton, Q.C., Minister of Transportation and Communications from C.M. Murray, Mayor of the Town of Mississauga*, July 24, 1973. Archives of Ontario, RG 3-49, tb 38, Davis General Correspondence, 1973.

4. S.B. McLaughlin, *100 Million Canadians: A Development Policy for Canada* (Mississauga: McLaughlin Planning and Research Institute, 1973), p. 7.

5. McLaughlin, *40 Million Places to Stand: A Development Policy for Ontario* (Mississauga: S.B. McLaughlin, 1975), p. 70.

6. McLaughlin, *100 Million Canadians*, p. 9.

7. Grant Clarkson, interview with the author, August 2000.

8. See, for example, "Election day is October 1—your responsibility to vote," *Review*, September 26, 1973.

9. See, for example, "Reeve wants Ward 4 seat," *Review*, September 5, 1973; and "Reeve now full time," *Review*, July 25, 1973.

10. These comments are made on recordings provided to the author by Bob Keeping. During the 1973 Mississauga election campaign, Keeping prepared and submitted news bulletins to various radio stations in the Toronto area.

11. "Streetsville mayor 'political warmonger,' says conservationist," *Toronto Star*, February 8, 1973.

12. Bob Keeping recordings.

13. Martin Dobkin, interview with the author, August 1999.

14. McCallion recalls this in Ron Duquette's documentary, *Hurricane Warning: The Life and Times of Hazel McCallion* (Ad-Venture Sight and Sound Production, 2001).

15. See, for example, "Town's transit system is a mess, Council told," *Globe and Mail*, January 9, 1973.

16. For an excellent summary of Dobkin's proposals, see "Policy Platform," *Booster*, August 7, 1973.

17. "Incumbents are wavering," *Mississauga Times*, September 3, 1973.

18. See, for example, Frank Touby, "Only three seats uncontested, election fever is rising," *Mississauga Times*, August 22, 1973.

19. Bob Keeping recordings.

20. For a good description of the candidates' styles, see Frank Touby, "Campbell breathes fire into sizzling campaign," *Times*, September 26, 1973.

21. "Dobkin roasts development policies," *Mississauga Times*, September 12, 1973.

22. *Review of Streetsville Official Plan, Report of Municipal Planning Consultants Co. Ltd., Part I*, July 16, 1973, Region of Peel Archives, 1996.065 AR, Box 4.

23. Jacobs' arguments are brilliantly articulated in her classic book *The Death and Life of Great American Cities* (New York: Random House, 1961).

24. This expression is used often by Mark E. Kann in *Middle Class Radicalism in Santa Monica* (Philadelphia: Temple University Press, 1986).

25. "Mayoralty race: Tense Dobkin versus Murray," *Mississauga Times*, September 19, 1973.

26. "T'ain't so, says Chic," *Review*, September 19, 1973.

27. "Mayoralty race: Tense Dobkin versus Murray," *Mississauga Times*, *op. cit.*

28. Jim Murray, interview with the author, August 2000.

29. Bob Keeping, interview with the author, August 1999.

30. The co-chairman in question was Rob Lawrie. See "Murray backers blink in disbelief," *Mississauga Times*, October 3, 1973.

31. Don Edwards, "Dobkin upsets Murray," *Mississauga News*, October 3, 1973; "Six new faces on new Council," *Mississauga News*, October 3, 1973; and Frank Touby, "Writing was on wall for Dobkin win," *Mississauga Times*, October 3, 1973.

32. May 10, 1973; Archives of Ontario, RG 3-49, tb 38, Davis General Correspondence, 1973.

CHAPTER 7: FAREWELL, TOWN OF STREETSVILLE

1. Promotional Committee file, Region of Peel Archives, 1994.063 AR, Box 5.

2. The press release and other documents pertaining to the closing ceremonies, including some of the Minutes of meetings, are in the Promotional Committee file, Region of Peel Archives, 1994.063 AR, Box 5.

3. There was considerable local press coverage before and after the events. For a good overview, see Jim Robinson, "Streetsville Days," *Mississauga News*, October 24, 1973 and "Streetsville Days," *Booster*, November 6, 1973.

4. Gloria Goodings, interview with the author, August 1999.

5. Emmaleen Sabourin, interview with the author, July 2000.

6. This prayer was also read at the final town council meeting. See appendix.

7. Jim Graham, interview with the author, July 2000.

8. Records of these discussions in late 1973 are contained in the file of the Mississauga City Organizational Committee, Clerk's Office, City of Mississauga. The information about Colley's salary was revealed in her

July 2000 interview with the author.

9. This is clear in correspondence between Davis and White dated September 11, 1973, Archives of Ontario, F 4151, tb 56, John White papers.

10. Archives of Ontario, RG 3-49, tb 38, Range B, Davis General Correspondence, 1973.

11. "Reeve Parsons quits business to serve public," *Mississauga News*, April 11, 1973.

12. Frank Touby, "Murray applauds appointment of Parsons, cites leadership," *Mississauga Times*, August 1, 1973.

13. Archives of Ontario, RG 3-49, tb 39, Range A, Davis General Correspondence, 1973.

14. The undated list is in the Archives of Ontario, RG 50-1, tb 24, Minister's Correspondence, 1973.

15. October 3, 1973, Archives of Ontario, F 4151, tb 10, John White papers.

16. Sabourin interview.

17. Considerable information on the police merger is contained in the *Peel Regional Police Force Work Committee Report* (Don Fletcher personal papers).

18. February 29, 1972; Archives of Ontario, RG 3-49, tb 39, Range A, Davis General Correspondence, 1972.

19. Jim Graham, interview with the author, July 2000.

20. The correspondence on this matter can be found in the Archives of Ontario, RG 19-131, tb 7. The correspondence from Farrow to Honey is dated August 21, 1973.

21. "Region to begin without fanfare," *Toronto Star*, December 27, 1973.

22. This remark was reported in the author's article "Dowling down memory lane," *Booster*, June 25, 1997.

AFTERWORD: A COMMUNITY IN TRANSITION

1. "The last meeting of council," *Review*, January 4, 1974.

2. See, for example, Peat, Marwick and Partners, *Mississauga Urban Development and Transportation Study: Evaluation and Recommendations*

(Toronto, 1975). See also City of Mississauga, *Draft Official Plan for the City of Mississauga* (1976).

3. For a good collection of articles on the inquiry and the political fallout surrounding it, see "Mississauga Judicial Inquiry Scrapbook" (LPC Scrapbook No. 50), Canadiana Room, Mississauga Central Library.

4. For an excellent discussion of the changing political mood in the "905" area, see John Lorinc, "The Story of Sprawl," *Toronto Life*, May 2001.

5. The judge's ruling is reprinted in full under the title "Mayor Hazel McCallion has her day in court," *Mississauga News,* July 28, 1982.

6. Archives of Ontario, RG 3-49, tb 9.

7. Doug Kennedy, interview with the author, July 2000.

8. See, for example, Andrew Sancton, *Merger Mania: The Assault on Local Government* (Montreal: McGill-Queen's University Press, 2000).

9. Archives of Ontario, RG 3-49, tb 34, Range A, Davis General Correspondence, 1974.

10. See, for example, Martin Dobkin, "Why your taxes increased," *Booster*, October 8, 1974. The increase for Streetsville residents was 18.68 percent.

11. Hazel McCallion, interview with the author, August 1999.

Index